Joyful Living

Lowell O. Erdahl

Revised and Expanded Edition
Of *Authentic Living*

CSS Publishing Company, Inc., Lima, Ohio

JOYFUL LIVING

Library of Congress Cataloging-in-Publication Data

Erdahl, Lowell O.
Joyful living / Lowell O. Erdahl.
p. cm.
ISBN 0-7880-1904-X (pbk. : alk. paper)
1. Devotional calendars. I. Erdahl, Lowell O. Authentic living. II. Title.
BV4811 .E68 2002
242'.2—dc21 2002004391

For more information about CSS Publishing Company resources, visit our website at www.csspub.com or e-mail us at custserv@csspub.com or call (800) 241-4056.

ISBN 0-7880-1904-X PRINTED IN U.S.A.

To the memory of E. Stanley Jones,
who helped me, and millions, see "the way."

Table Of Contents

Introduction to the Original Edition

Each of us hungers to be fully human. We yearn to be true to ourselves and to others. I believe that the secret of such authentic living has been revealed, and that it involves something we can call "an adventure of abandonment." These pages seek to enable that life — the life we are designed to live. If this purpose seems pretentious, I can only say, "Come and see" (John 1:46). Look to the promises of God; abandon to him, and see if this is life in fullness.

As in an unfolding venture, the material is presented in daily readings. Since there is a theme for each week, the book may also be read in weekly sections or straight through as the reader prefers.

E. Stanley Jones, to whose memory this book is gratefully dedicated, spoke to my condition. I commend his writings and suggest *The Way* (Abingdon, 1946) and *Selections from E. Stanley Jones* (Abingdon, 1972) as excellent summaries of his message. Others who helped shape the convictions of these pages include Martin Luther, John Wesley, Harry Emerson Fosdick, Paul Scherer, and Paul Tournier. Oswald Chambers' emphasis on the centrality of "reckless abandon to God" has been especially significant. Personal thanks go to Professors Paul Sponheim and William Smith of Luther Theological Seminary, and to Pastors Ted Vinger and Myrwood Bagne for their frequent encouragement, and to Evelyn Brisson and Sue Wolf for their kindness and skill in preparing the manuscript.

The original edition, published with the title *Authentic Living*, provided readings for fifteen weeks. The revised edition has been expanded to sixteen weeks.

Introduction to the Revised Edition

Since *Authentic Living* went out of print several years ago many have hoped for a new edition, and I am pleased that CSS Publishing has acted to provide it. I have been grateful for the CSS paperback edition of my book *The Lonely House, Strength for Times of Loss*, and now express appreciation to Tim Runk, Stan Purdum, and Teresa Rhoads at CSS for their initiative and helpfulness in creating this new edition, and to Maxine Enfield for preparing the additions and revisions.

There are three major changes from the original edition that was published by Abingdon. Most obvious is the new title which I believe more specifically expresses the central theme of the book. The second most obvious change is the addition of a week of readings that deal with "Life In Our Larger Families" which is a concern that has become increasingly important to me.

The third major revision may be less obvious. It has involved an attempt to remove the use of sexist language which many, including myself, now find offensive. I respect the feelings of those who believe that this cleansing should have been even more extensive. The publisher and I have agreed to retain many references to God as "he" and hope that those for whom this causes distress will have mercy on us.

This little book attempts to share convictions that are extremely important and meaningful to me, and if some of them have meaning and give joy to those who read these pages I will be deeply grateful.

The Joy We Seek

"Joy," says Rollo May, "is the goal of life." But in what does this joy consist? He answers: "To the extent that we ... fulfill our potentialities as persons, we experience the profoundest joy to which the human being is heir ... Joy is the emotion which accompanies our fulfilling our natures as human beings."

Dr. May cites the simple illustration of a child learning to walk. After many falls she finally succeeds and "laughs with gratification." Such is true at every level of life. We, too, laugh or smile with joyful gratification when, in some way, we "fulfill our natures" as human beings.

Here then is our chief need and deepest desire — not a frantic pursuit of joy, which in such quest always eludes us, but to "fulfill our natures," to live authentically, to be true to ourselves, to "fulfill our potentialities as persons." For ourselves and for all we love, we want the joy of authentic living, and in these pages seek to share the open secret of such life.

Prayer: Enable us, O Lord, to know the joy of fulfilling our natures. In Jesus' name. Amen.

Thought: Joy is a by-product of authentic living.

Week One, Day Two

Psalm 1:1-6
John 10:1-10

Life In All Its Fullness

We seek the joy of authentic living. But where do we learn, and how do we live, this life? Some ways of living lead to misery. "There is a way that seems right to a person, but its end is the way to death" (Proverbs 14:12 NRSV). Many, said Fosdick, live like a man who caught the wrong bus. Intending to go to Detroit, he ended in Kansas City. So we, while intending our happiness, often live in ways that bring us to regret. Our roads and not our desires determine the destination.

The central conviction of this book is that authentic living is both revealed and enabled by Jesus Christ. He is the supreme revelation of authentic humanity. In him we see the persons we are born to be and the lives we are meant to live. But more than this, in him we also see the presence and the power of God who alone enables this venture of living.

Jesus came not just to make us religious, but to give us life. "I have come," he said, "that they may have life, and may have it in all its fullness" (John 10:10 REB). In these weeks together we seek to share that life.

Prayer: Thank you, Lord, for coming in Christ to give us authentic life. Lead us now to live it. In Jesus' name. Amen.

Thought: I will to live — Christ wills to give me life. He and I must get together.

Imposed Or Exposed?

Many people seem to regard Christianity as another religion imposed upon life, and insofar as Christianity is understood to be a system of ritual, belief, and behavior, they may be correct. Too often during the 2,000 years of its history, Christianity has been just that — an imposition, a foreign faith forced upon life, a religious burden to be borne by the faithful in the hope of meriting heaven. When understood in this way, "Christianity" is an enemy of Christ that can be rightly described as the "opiate of the people." But Jesus came not to impose religion upon us, but to expose the reality of authentic humanness and to enable us to follow him in living that life.

Jesus did not come to persuade us to become "Christian" in the sense of being practitioners of a religious system called "Christianity." He came to enable us to be more fully human — to live whole, harmonious, authentic lives. Insofar as Christianity is the living of that life, it is not an imposition of religion, but an expression of authentic humanity revealed and enabled by Jesus Christ.

Prayer: Author of Life, enable us to be true to your design. Keep us in harmony with you and with ourselves. In Jesus' name. Amen.

Thought: Jesus does not impose religion. He exposes and enables life.

Week One, Day Four John 14:1-11
Acts 9:2; 19:9, 23; 22:4; 24:14-22

The Way

"The Christian way," says E. Stanley Jones, is not "a way" but "*The* Way — the way for everything and everybody, everywhere and in every circumstance." This way is written not only "in the text of scripture, but also in the texture of the world."

Since first reading Jones' exposition of "the Way," I have grown increasingly sure of the validity of its central insight. I believe that Jones is right: "The Christian way is the natural way — the way we are made to live. Everything else is unnatural." When we live against Christ, we are living not only against God and the Bible, but also against ourselves and all that gives life meaning and beauty. Living in Christ, we are in harmony not only with heaven, but also with the heart of our humanity and the heart of the universe.

Such a claim can hardly be accepted on one person's authority, but it can be tested in the laboratory of living. Millions have heard Jesus say: "I am the way, and the truth, and the life" (John 14:6), and to the extent they have trusted and followed him they have found it to be true. In these weeks, we seek to see this way, to know this truth, and to live this life.

Prayer: O Lord, save us from living against the grain of life. Bring our lives in line with reality. In Jesus' name. Amen.

Thought: Christ is the Way — the Way I am designed to live.

Week One, Day Five

Colossians 1:15-17
John 15:1-8

Created For Christ

Colossians says of Christ, "All things were created through him and for him ... and in him all things hold together" (1:16, 17). Can this be true? Is Christ our native air? Are we created for him as fish for the sea, birds for the air, and leaves for the sun? Are we designed for Christ as our eyes are made for light and our ears for sound? Are we, when living contrary to Christ, like fish out of water, separated from the reality in which we are created to live?

Imagine a goldfish having just leaped free from its bowl. As it flips on the floor, it may think to itself "Now I am free! Free from the water in which I have been trapped so long! Free to really live!" But it is a short-lived freedom. Apart from water, a fish is free only to struggle and then to die. Such, says Jesus, is our situation: "Abide in me, and I in you. As the branch cannot bear fruit by itself, unless it abides in me.... For apart from me you can do nothing" (John 15:4, 5). This statement is either an outrageous lie or a fundamental fact of life. Can it be true — in Christ we thrive, out of Christ we wilt, wither, and die?

Prayer: O Christ, keep us connected to the source of our life. Give us faith to abide in your life-giving Spirit. In your name. Amen.

Thought: In Christ "all things hold together" — out of Christ all things fall apart.

Week One, Day Six

Hebrews 11:23-28
Romans 6:20-23

Beyond The Obvious

If we thrive in Christ and wither apart from him, why do the wicked often prosper? Why is there joy in the lives of people who make no confession of Christ?

We need a long-term view. There is beauty in a cut flower, but it is dying. So also there are pleasures in wickedness, but they are "fleeting" (Hebrews 11:25). Sin leaves a hangover. Ways of living contrary to the way we see in Jesus are not just sinful, but, in the long run, harmful for us and for all with whom we live.

We also remember that some things called "Christian" may be contrary to Christ, while others not so labeled may be in harmony with him. Some "non-Christians" may live the Christian way more truly than do some "Christians." In Jesus we see that to be religious is not necessarily to be a follower of "the Way." What matters is not outward observance or verbal confession, but vital attitudes of the heart. As there are pseudo-Christians in the church, there may be anonymous Christians outside. Being in a henhouse does not make one a hen, nor does being in a church automatically make one a Christian. A Christian lives "the Way."

Prayer: O God, save us from fleeting pleasures that bring long-term misery. Lead us to life with joy abiding. In Jesus' name. Amen.

Thought: Beyond face and form, God sees the heart.

On The Side Of Life

Looking to Jesus Christ, we dare believe that God is on the side of life. He created us for abundant life. He wills to bless us. Does something enrich and ennoble life, give beauty, meaning, and joy? Then God is for it, and is working now to sustain and to enlarge it.

Jesus invites our trust that no matter who or what may be against us, God is for us and that nothing "in all creation will be able to separate us" from his love (Romans 8:39). How differently we live when sustained by this promise! There are still plenty of problems, but now we are enabled to live with confidence and hope.

Since God is for life, he is inherently against all that is anti-life. The wrath of God against evil is an expression of his love. We cannot care for another person and be indifferent to actions that hurt the one we love. Nor can God love people and affirm life without holy anger against all that hinders the joy of his children.

Prayer: Thank you, God, for the gift of life. Whatever may be against us, assure us that you are for us. In Jesus' name. Amen.

Thought: Since God is for us, what matters who is against us?

The Stream Of Grace

Conflicting forces vie for control of our lives. We sometimes feel like a battleground on which opposing armies struggle to dominate our wills and decide our destinies. Some of these forces seem demonic — fears, dark moods of hatred, feelings of hopelessness and despair. Though our scientific thinking may reject such thoughts, we sometimes feel like persons possessed by evil spirits seeking to destroy us.

Evil is real, but God is more real. Whatever works against us, Jesus promises that a mighty life-giving Presence — an energizing and enabling field of force — is ever present, ever at work for our health and wholeness. This is the presence of the Living God, the Holy Spirit, the Living Spirit of Christ.

Like little boats on a great river, our lives are driven and tossed by surface winds and crosscurrents. But whatever the surface storms, Jesus reveals the main flow of the river to be a mighty stream of grace — a powerful love and the loving power — bearing us onward and upward toward fullness of life.

Prayer: O Lord, give us courage to trust that your graceful presence is the most real and mighty force in the universe. In Jesus' name. Amen.

Thought: Whatever the storms, the stream of grace sustains me still.

Week Two, Day Two

Psalm 103:6-14
1 John 4:7-19

God Loves You!

It may seem impersonal and abstract to speak of the Divine Presence as an energizing, enabling field of force or a sustaining stream of grace. Any analogy of the Living God is at best suggestive of the mighty, mysterious reality to which it witnesses. To such analogies we must quickly add the dimension of personal, caring love which is the dominant theme of biblical witness.

The central message of scripture and of Christ is that God loves and wills to bless us. His greatness is revealed not only in the power that sets the stars in space, but above all in his individual care for each of his children. "Even the hairs of your head," said Jesus, "are all numbered" (Matthew 10:30).

The thought of God deeply caring for each of his children boggles the mind and staggers the imagination. Pause and ponder this promise: the Creator, the ground and source of all life, personally cares for you! It seems beyond belief, yet the words and deeds of Jesus say, in effect, "Trust me, it is true — God loves you and wills to bless your life!"

Prayer: Lord of Love, thank you for knowing us by name and caring for each of us. Deepen our trust. In Jesus' name. Amen.

Thought: The Almighty cares for me? Jesus says, "Believe it!"

Week Two, Day Three

Psalm 27:7-14
1 John 3:19-24

More Than We Love Ourselves

Many live with abundant self-love. Yet, as Luther liked to say, "God loves us more than we love ourselves." He is more concerned with our welfare than we are. No matter how great our self-love, God loves us more. More than we wish to be blessed, he wills to bless us.

And when we hate and despise ourselves, he still loves us and strives to bring us joy. Others may cease to love us. Father and mother may forsake us. Husbands, wives, children, friends may give up on us and turn away; we may give up on ourselves. Yet in Christ — we are assured that God still cares and works to bless.

Make believe, if need be, that Almighty God now cares for you more than you care for yourself. Imagine yourself held and sustained by such a love. Was Jesus crazy to live with this faith and to invite us to share it? He seems so sane and sound in everything else. Maybe it's really true — God loves us more than we love ourselves!

Prayer: O Lord, thank you that the greatness of your love is not limited by the littleness of our ability to comprehend or believe. Stretch our imaginations toward the vastness of your care. In Jesus' name. Amen.

Thought: When I love me much, God loves me more!

"Just As I Am"

"Isn't there some catch to the love of God? Don't I have to do something or stop doing something to get God to love me? Do I dare believe that God loves me now with all my faults and doubts, and with all the peculiarities I'm glad others don't know about? Certainly I must change something first — then God will love me."

We may think that we must first repent and give up our sins, first believe and deny our doubts, and then after we have taken the first step, God will love us. But that is not the sequence we see in Jesus. "We love, because he first loved us" (1 John 4:19). Jesus first loved and welcomed the woman taken in adultery; only then did he say, "Go, and do not sin again" (John 8:11). God does not love us because we repent and believe. We can repent and believe because God loves us — *now* in our impenitence and unbelief!

Prayer:

Just as I am, though tossed about
With many a conflict, many a doubt,
Fightings and fears within, without,
O Lamb of God, I come, I come!

Just as I am, thou wilt receive,
Wilt welcome, pardon, cleanse, relieve;
Because thy promise I believe,
O Lamb of God, I come, I come!
Amen.

Thought: Loved now, "Just as I am"? Yes! Just as I am!

One Thing We Cannot Do

"Do you know the most important thing you said in these ten years?" asked a parishioner of his departing pastor. "What was that?" "You told us that we can't do anything to get God to stop loving us!"

We can't stop God from loving us any more than we can stop the sun from shining. The sun doesn't shine because we are good or stop when we are bad. It shines whether we know it or believe it or like it. So also with the love of God — God loves us because that's the way God is: "God is love" (1 John 4:8, 16). In Christ, God says in effect: "I love you now and will love you forever. Nothing you or anyone else can ever do will stop me from loving you."

We can, of course, live as if the sun were not shining. We can board up the windows and live in the dark. Yet our lives would still be sustained by the sun's warmth and fed by the work of its light. So too, we can live as if God did not love us. We can believe ourselves to be living in a cold and empty universe. But like the disbeliever in the sun, we would still be sustained by the love we deny. We'd miss the joy of basking in the warmth of his grace, but God would still be the source of our life.

Prayer: O God, teach us not to flee, but to rejoice in the sunshine of your grace. In Jesus' name. Amen.

Thought: Since I can't stop his loving, I will let God love me to the full.

A Copernican Revolution

Before Copernicus, most people believed that the sun and stars revolved around the earth. When Copernicus taught that the earth is not at the center of the universe, many protested, and it was years before his "revolutionary" way of understanding reality was universally accepted.

Most of us need a Copernican revolution in our thinking about ourselves and God. We see ourselves at the center of the universe and regard everything as revolving around us. We are especially prone to think that our life and salvation are totally dependent upon what we do. Our hopes center in our own ability and achievements.

Jesus invites us to see ourselves differently. First, to see that we are not at the center of the universe. God is the center, and each of us is only one of his children. Second, and of equal importance, to see that our life and salvation do not depend upon our ability and achievement, but upon God who creates and saves us without our help or contribution. It is all "by grace ... through faith; and this is not your own doing, it is the gift of God" (Ephesians 2:8).

Prayer: O God, give us eyes of faith to see you at the center and ourselves as your children. In Jesus' name. Amen.

Thought: God does not help us save ourselves; he saves us without our help.

Eccentric?

A wheel or person that is off-center is called "eccentric." When centered in ourselves we are eccentric. To center our hopes in ourselves and to rely upon our strength alone may seem the natural way to live. But if Jesus is right, we were never meant to live that way. As Copernicus revealed the physical reality of the universe, so Jesus reveals the ultimate reality of human life. We are created by God to live by his love and power. All other living is alien to our design and contrary to our essential nature.

Many of us, as E. Stanley Jones liked to say, have been thoroughly "naturalized to the unnatural." We are like addicts, who are so hooked on harmful drugs that they suffer withdrawal symptoms when the drugs are removed. Though neither natural nor healthful, drug dependence may seem so to the person addicted. So also, we who are "hooked" on a self-centered, self-saving way of life may be unaware of how unnatural, unhealthy, and eccentric our living really is. Yet something in us yearns for authentic, joyful life, and the call of Jesus bids us seek and live it.

Prayer: O Lord, lead us to live on-center. Naturalize us to life in harmony with our essential nature. In Jesus' name. Amen.

Thought: Centered in self, I am eccentric. Centered in Christ, I am on-center.

Week Three, Day One

Psalm 42:1-11
John 12:31-32

Lured By Love

As sailors feel the lure of the sea calling them to launch out into the deep, we feel the lure of the love of God beckoning us to leave the shores of self-saving living and to venture ourselves upon the sea of his grace. Like young eagles perched on the nest, we open our wings of faith and feel the lift of the wind of God's Spirit. We fear to let go, and yet the thrill of the wind tells of a soaring life of freedom and joy beyond the nest. An instinct for flight awakens within us. We yearn to be swept up by the wind of God's Spirit.

Centuries ago the Psalmist told of our experience: "As a hart longs for flowing streams, so longs my soul for thee, O God. My soul thirsts for God, for the living God" (Psalm 42:1, 2). Saint Augustine also speaks for us all: "Our hearts are restless until they find their rest in thee." We are designed to live by the love of God. As an eagle is created for the sky, and has wings for the wind, we are created for God and have wings of faith to be opened to the wind of his Spirit.

Prayer: Holy Spirit of God, by the moving power of your living presence lift us all to new levels of authentic, joyful living. Give us courage to launch out and live. In Jesus' name. Amen.

Thought: The whispering wind of God's Spirit lures me to live by his love.

Two Ways Of Living

There are hundreds of religions in the world, but according to Jesus essentially only two ways of life. One way is "self-saving," the other is "self-losing." Note the outcome of each: "For those who want to save their life will lose it, and those who lose their life for my sake will save it" (Luke 9:24 NRSV).

Jesus' words reveal a fact of life. When we live by "attachment" — clinging to life, to self, to people, to things — we are on the self-saving way that leads to loss of the life we seek. When we live by "abandonment" — letting go, trusting that we are loved, and lifted by the stream of grace — then we are on the self-losing way that leads to life in fullness.

Assured by Christ of the living, loving presence of the divine Spirit, we give ourselves away — in trust to the love of God and with love to the lives of people. As we follow Jesus in this adventure of abandonment, we enter a new way of living which is nothing less than the authentic life we are created to live.

Prayer: O Lord, save us from every form of futile self-saving. Give us courage to let go and live. In Jesus' name. Amen.

Thought: Christ calls us to give ourselves away — in trust to God and with love to people.

Week Three, Day Three

John 12:20-27
Galatians 2:19-21

From God To Grain

In Christ on the cross, we see God acting in self-giving love. Then we remember the words of Jesus: "Truly, truly, I say to you, unless a grain of wheat falls into the earth and dies, it remains alone; but if it dies, it bears much fruit" (John 12:24). From God to grain, the principle is the same; self-saving dies, self-losing lives and is life-giving.

When we grasp at life to save it for ourselves, we kill it. We are like a child who hugs his puppy to death. As we fearfully try to keep the life we prize, we are cutting off life's most vital circulation — the inward flow of God's love to us and the outward flow of our love to others. Without the free circulation of that love we can exist but cannot fully live.

"The call to follow Christ," said Dietrich Bonhoeffer, "is a call to come and die." That is true — it is a call to die to self as "god." But that death to self as god is the birth of self as an authentic human being. Like the grain of wheat that falls into the earth, this death is birth to new life and fruitfulness.

Prayer: O God, from the cross to the seed, we begin to see your way. Lead us now to live it. In Jesus' name. Amen.

Thought: We are created in the image of a self-giving God.

Week Three, Day Four

Luke 12:22-31
Mark 10:13-16
1 Corinthians 7:29-31

A Good Word For Loose Living

There is one kind of loose living which comes commended by Christ. "Do not be anxious about your life, what you shall eat, nor about your body, what you shall put on ... nor be of anxious mind" (Luke 12:22-29). Jesus invites us to live as "loosely" as the birds of the air and the flowers of the field. They do not fret or frantically cling to life, yet God cares for them. "How much more," says Jesus, "will he clothe you — you of little faith' " (Luke 12:28 NRSV).

Such simple pictures and promises may seem an insult to our intelligence. How, in a world like this, can mature, reasonable people live with the native trust of birds and flowers? How can we who have come of age live with the confidence of children? One fact makes such trust possible. We are the children of God, whom he loves and wants to bless. If this is true, childlike faith is hardheaded realism. If God loves and wills to bless us and we do not trust him, we are not just sinners, we are fools!

Prayer: O Lord, held tightly in the grasp of your grace, give us courage to live loosely with everything else. In Jesus' name. Amen.

Thought: We are created not for tension, but for trust.

Week Three, Day Five

Matthew 7:13-14
Hebrews 11:1-12

Riding In God's Wheelbarrow!

An old story tells of a tightrope walker whose feature performance was to roll a wheelbarrow across the high wire near the roof of the circus tent. As he prepared to rehearse his act, the manager of the circus asked a helper, "Do you think he can do it?" "I have no doubt," said the helper. "He is the greatest tightrope walker in the world. I am sure he can do it!" "I am glad you feel that way," said the manager, "because I want you to ride in the wheelbarrow!"

Living with faith is really riding in God's wheelbarrow! It is not just believing things about God, or telling about how great he is. These have their place, but in themselves they are not faith. Faith is entrusting our lives to the promised presence and power of God. It is "letting go" of all to which we cling and "letting God" be the source and strength of our lives.

The faith-life is a daily adventure of almost reckless abandonment to the promised presence of God. As we "let go and let God" we enter the pilgrimage of the self-losing life. This is a frightening venture. Who knows where it will lead? Yet we move ahead, assured by Christ that we have set our feet upon "the way ... that leads to life" (Matthew 7:14).

Prayer: O Lord, give us courage to ride in your wheelbarrow. In Jesus' name. Amen.

Thought: Letting go, I let God give me life.

Week Three, Day Six

Deuteronomy 33:27a
Matthew 11:28-30
Matthew 28:16-20

Trying Versus Trusting

Many say, "If at first you don't succeed, try, try again." But Jesus invites us to live differently — not by trying but by trusting, not by hanging on but by letting go.

E. Stanley Jones helps us see the way:

> *Cease from struggling. Don't try to do this yourself; let Him do it ... You will be tempted to struggle and try instead of relax and trust and receive. "When I gave all trying over, simply trusting I was blessed." ... As long as you are trying, you are on the basis of yourself; but the moment you begin to trust, you are on the basis of Christ.*

Jones says that "faith is pure receptivity." Luther spoke of faith as pure passivity. Faith is resting in the arms of God. Faith does nothing but let God do all he has promised. Faith is being receptively passive toward God's action.

Passive faith is only one side of Christian life. Active love is the other side. We work, but first we learn to trust. Jesus first says, "Come to me ... and I will give you rest" (Matthew 11:28). Then he says, "Go for me, and get to work." First the passivity of trust, then the activity of love.

Prayer: O Lord, lead us to rest and to work, to be passive in trust and then to be active in love. In Jesus' name. Amen.

Thought: First I will trust, then I will try.

Week Three, Day Seven

Luke 11:5-13
Ephesians 2:8-10

"First Receive – Then Respond"

E. Stanley Jones says that

> *... the two laws of life are receptivity and response. But first* receptivity. *Many reverse this and try to respond, respond, to try, to do. No, first receive — receive by a quiet appropriating faith. Then you will respond, naturally and out of the resources which receptivity brings.*

The faith to which we are lured by the love of God is both a trustful dependence upon God and a welcoming receptivity toward God. It is openness to receive the good God wills for us, and especially the gift of his healing Holy Spirit.

Trust and receptivity, being held and being healed — these are the vital beginnings of Christian life. But more — they are the ongoing dynamic and vital center, not only of Christian life but of authentic human existence. And to begin such life, nothing is demanded of us — no religious or moral or intellectual achievement. It is all of grace, from God who woos us with a winning love. The mood, as Paul Scherer said, is more like courtship than the courtroom. Through Christ we are given the confidence of being loved.

Prayer: Spirit of God, give us both faith to trust and openness to receive. Thank you for being with us and within us. In Jesus' name. Amen.

Thought: Wooed by God's love, I yield to be held and to be healed.

Week Four, Day One

Exodus 20:1-6
Psalm 86:1-12
Isaiah 37:14-20

Abandonment?

If authentic living is "an adventure of abandonment," in what does this "abandonment" consist? To abandon is (1) "to give up ... to give over or surrender completely," and (2) "to yield one's self up without attempt at restraint; as to abandon one's self to grief."

This week we concentrate on how Christ calls us to abandon false gods and to abandon ourselves to God. Next week we will consider how Christ also sends us to love with abandon.

The real god in our lives is that to which we look for our life and strength. Our god, for example, may not be "Father, Son, and Holy Spirit" but "Me, Myself, and I." When our central trust is in ourselves, self has become god, and we are worshiping an idol. The self is good, but it is not God. Most idols are not bad things but good things put in God's place. One alone is God. He is the only God there is — beside him there is no other.

Prayer: O Lord, save us from putting the temporal in place of the eternal, the good in place of God. In Jesus' name. Amen.

Thought: Letting go of "gods," I let God be God — for me.

Deuteronomy 5:6-10
Acts 14:8-18

Resigned?

Someone said, "The best day in my life was when I resigned from being chair of the board of the universe." Most of us are less pretentious, but we are all tempted to be chair of the board of our own lives. Such thinking is out of touch with reality. Whatever our positions or power, each of us is a human being and not a god. To live like a god is as foolish as it is sinful. To put such trust in ourselves is like building a house on the ice of a northern lake and expecting to live in it year around. As sure as the sun shines, that house is going down.

In the long run, we live very poorly as make-believe gods, but we can live amazingly well as human beings loved of God and sustained by his Spirit. To give up pretending to be god is not to be humiliated, but to be released from a silly sham. It also frees us to turn our trust to the only God there is — the God with whom we are designed to live and in whom alone we live authentically.

Prayer: O God, forgive us for trying to take your place. Give us the faith and wisdom to let you be God and to let ourselves be authentic human beings. In Jesus' name. Amen.

Thought: Having failed as a "god," I can, by God's grace, succeed as a human being.

Week Four, Day Three

Psalm 90:1, 2
Hebrews 13:5-8

The Clinging Syndrome

Stanley Jones told of two people at prayer. One prayed, "Lord, give me the strength to hang on"; the other, "Lord, give me the faith to let go." A world of difference separates those prayers and those lives.

Many of us live the clinging syndrome. Like a frightened child clutching a security blanket, we cling to people, pleasures, money, and things. Above all, as D. R. Davies put it, "We cling to the last rag of self as a virtuous woman clings to her last garment." The fault is not in the "thing" we grasp but in our clinging to it as if it were the source of life itself.

Yet you may wonder, what else can we do? Imagine yourself falling over a cliff on a pitch-black night and clinging to a branch with dread that the canyon floor is far below. Hanging on seems the only alternative to disaster. To be told to let go seems absurd. Yet if the darkness hides a mountain road inches beneath your toes, letting go is safe to do.

As we cling to something for survival, Jesus assures us that the rock of God's presence is beneath our feet. Indeed, his hands of love enfold us now! "Let go," says Jesus; "God will not let you down!"

Prayer: O Lord, give us courage to live not by clinging but with confidence in your presence and power. In Jesus' name. Amen.

Thought: When I let go, I fall into the loving arms of God.

Week Four, Day Four

Psalm 94:16-22
Luke 15:3-7

Let Go Of God

Let go of God? This may seem strange, but to some, among whom may be the most religious, it may be one of the most important invitations of your life.

"Raise your hands," said a revival preacher, "and get a good hold on God." That is a noble sentiment, but it is not of grace. Authentic living is not clinging to God as if we could hang onto him. It centers in confidence that God holds us and will hold us forever.

By way of example, think of how we learn to swim when we quit trying to hold ourselves up and begin to trust that we are held by the water. Or recall the childhood experience of being held in strong arms of tender love. Within the safety of that warm embrace we could relax, rest, and even sleep in peace.

So also we need not cling to God, but can let go and rest in his love, secure in the safety of his mighty arms. It is as in Jesus' parable (Luke 15:3-7): the sheep does not cling to the shepherd — the shepherd carries the sheep.

Prayer: O Lord our God, save us from frantically trying to hang on to you. Hold us now and forever in your mighty love. In Jesus' name. Amen.

Thought: "O love that wilt not let me go, I rest my weary soul in thee."

Week Four, Day Five

Psalm 145:1-21
Jude 24, 25

Let Go To God

As we let go *of* God we also let go *to* God, letting him hold us in his love. Sometimes we are like white-knuckled airline passengers who are afraid to relax and trust the plane. They are being carried, but they feel as if they have to hold themselves up. One such passenger was asked, "How did you like the flight?" "It was all right," he replied. "But I never let my weight down once."

When hiking west, a frontiersman came to an ice-covered river. Fearful of thin ice, he began to creep across on his hands and knees. Halfway over he was startled by noise from beyond the bend. Looking up he was relieved to see a team of horses coming down the middle of the river pulling a sled loaded with logs. Joyfully, he jumped to his feet, confident that the ice, strong enough to carry that team, could easily support him.

We need neither hold ourselves up, nor creep fearfully through life. We are being carried by God, who promises never to let us down. With joyful abandon we rest in God, trusting him to hold us forever.

Prayer: O Lord, deliver us from fearful creeping and give us confidence and courage befitting your children. In Jesus' name. Amen.

Thought: My little weight is not too much for God.

Week Four, Day Six

Mark 5:1-20
Romans 6:12-19

Letting Down Our Defenses

In letting go to God we also abandon the defenses we set against the invasion of his Spirit. Our lives are sometimes like a fortress with walls of stone on every side. We fear that our defenses will collapse and that we will be invaded by the forces intent to destroy us.

There is ground for such fear. Powers of evil seek to invade and inhabit our lives. But there is one more mighty than they. Whatever demonic "spirits" may seek to destroy us, the divine Spirit wills and works to enter and give us life.

Therefore, our greater danger is not that our defenses will fall, but that they will stand, and in standing shut out not only our foes but our truest friend. As we let down our defenses we open ourselves to the life-giving Spirit of Christ.

We pray: "Come Holy Spirit, enter in, cleanse and heal and make me whole. Fill me with your presence and drive out the demonic power of sin, sickness, and every evil." Then we say, "Thank you," trusting that God is already at work answering our prayers.

Prayer: Healing Holy Spirit, we open our lives to the invasion of your presence. Transform us from the inside out. Make us clean and give us strength for your service. In Jesus' name. Amen.

Thought: As I abandon my defenses, I say, "Welcome," to God.

Week Four, Day Seven

Luke 12:15-21
1 Corinthians 3:21-23
2 Corinthians 6:3-10

All Things Are Yours

In the adventure of abandonment, we travel with no security in ourselves, no possessions we can call our own, no people who can guarantee our safety. We have nothing that lets us say with the rich fool in Jesus' parable, "Soul, you have ample goods laid up for many years; take your ease, eat, drink, be merry" (Luke 12:19-20).

But looking to Jesus we dare to trust that we belong to God and that he will keep us forever. Having nothing in ourselves, we now possess everything in him: his love, his power, his live-giving presence. "We live," says Paul, "as having nothing, and yet possessing everything" (2 Corinthians 6:9, 10); and again, "All things are yours ... and you are Christ's; and Christ is God's" (1 Corinthians 3:21-23).

In Christ we have everything we need. We have only abandoned a false and futile way of life. In place of grasping, we live by grace. Having nothing in ourselves, we have all things in Christ.

Prayer: Save us, O Lord, from the poverty of being rich only in things. Give us instead the unsearchable riches of Christ. In his name. Amen.

Thought: When I have all I need, what more do I need?

Week Five, Day One

Galatians 5:1-15
1 John 4:7-12

Liberated To Love

Authentic living is an adventure of "letting go and letting God." Jesus says: "Set your troubled hearts at rest. Trust in God always; trust also in me" (John 14:1 NEB). That "always" reminds us that receptive trust is continual. We never live beyond our need of the love of God. His grace is as essential to life in fullness as air is for physical survival.

But trustful receptivity is only one side of authentic living. Even as we let go of our idols and let God be God, we also give ourselves with abandon to care for people. With assurance of God's blessing and strength, Jesus sends us into the world to live with self-forgetful, self-giving love.

"Life," says Paul Sponheim, "is gift, but it is task, as well." In Christ we rest and work at the same time. As a ship rests in the sea and works to reach its destination, we, too, simultaneously rest in the love of God and work to give life to others. Freed from having to lift ourselves, we are liberated to love.

Prayer: O Lord, save us from being corks — afloat but doing nothing. Make us like ships — at work for others while at rest in you. In Jesus' name. Amen.

Thought: Grace frees me from futile self-saving and for fruitful self-giving.

Week Five, Day Two

Luke 6:27-36
Ephesians 2:8-10

Designed For Good Deeds

Created to live by the grace of God, we are also "designed" for doing good. Paul sums up both sides of authentic living: "By his grace you are saved, through trusting in him; it is not your own doing ... We are God's handiwork, created in Christ Jesus to devote ourselves to the good deeds for which God has designed us" (Ephesians 2:8-10 NEB).

"By his grace ... through trusting him" — this is the side of passive, receptive faith. "To devote ourselves to the good deeds for which God has designed us" — this is the side of active, caring love. Like breathing in and breathing out, faith and love go together.

No human capacity is more significant than our ability to receive and give love. We need not have great minds or great bodies to be greatly loved and greatly loving. Some people, hurt deeply, find it difficult to trust or love anyone. To escape disappointment we may withdraw from God and people. Yet whatever hinders our faith and love, God is at work to heal our broken hearts and to help us trust and care again.

Prayer: O Lord, heal us of hurts that hinder our faith and limit our love. In Jesus' name. Amen.

Thought: To be loved and to love — this is my design and my destiny.

Week Five, Day Three

Philippians 4:10-13
Colossians 1:24-29

Grace And Gumption

When asked the secret of his zestful life, E. Stanley Jones gave primary credit to "grace and gumption." That's quite a combination: "grace" — the forgiving, energizing presence of God, and "gumption" — personal initiative, get-up-and-go. Vital people like Stanley Jones illustrate what can happen when God's grace and human gumption get together.

Grace and gumption were also wedded in the Apostle Paul. Of his mission to "present each one of you as a mature member of Christ's body," Paul says, "To this end I am toiling strenuously with all the energy and power of Christ at work in me" (Colossians 1:28, 29 REB). Here is personal striving (gumption) sustained by divine energy (grace). In weakness Paul found strength in God's "sufficient" grace (2 Corinthians 12:9). Empowered by God's graceful presence, Paul can say: "I have learned the secret of facing ... abundance and want. I can do all things in him who strengthens me" (Philippians 4:12-13).

Some live with neither grace nor gumption. Others have much gumption but know little of grace. Still others trust grace but show little gumption. Then some, like Paul and Stanley Jones, live by grace and with gumption. That's real living!

Prayer: O Lord, give us faith and love to live by grace and with gumption. In Jesus' name. Amen.

Thought: Inspired by God, I will perspire for people.

Week Five, Day Four

John 13:31-35
1 Corinthians 13:1-14

The Mark Of Maturity

Love is the mark of Christianity. "By this," says Jesus, "everyone will know that you are my disciples if you have love for one another" (John 13:35 NRSV). But love is also the mark of maturity. Speaking of love, Paul says, "When I became an adult, I gave up childish ways" (1 Corinthians 13:11 NRSV). Again, authentic Christianity and authentic humanity come together.

Since our love is imperfect, we are all, in some measure, inauthentic, unfulfilled, subhuman people. Thankfully, our eternal hope depends not on our perfect love but on God who "loved us and sent his Son to be the expiation for our sins" (1 John 4:10). But the next verse goes on: "Beloved, if God so loved us, we also ought to love one another" (1 John 4:11)

We need not stay as we are. By God's power we can grow toward the likeness of Christ. "We need not," said Fosdick, "be great in ourselves to stand for something great." As an ordinary person can carry a great flag, we can all carry the colors of Christ. Weak and sinful as we are, we can be used by a great God to share his love.

Prayer: O Lord, love us into loving, forgive us into forgiving, use us to carry the colors of Christ. In his name. Amen.

Thought: Love reveals our Christianity, our maturity, our humanity.

Week Five, Day Five

Mark 12:28-34
Romans 12:3-13

Humility

Someone said that "humility is not thinking less of ourselves than of others; it is not thinking of ourselves one way or the other at all." Humility is not self-depreciation but self-forgetfulness.

Periodic self-examination is a necessity; perpetual self-preoccupation is a curse. Self-examination is an occasional glance in the mirror. Self-preoccupation is endlessly looking to see if we are beautiful enough.

Assured of God's love, we need not pay excessive attention to ourselves. We seek to keep fit for God's service, but need not worry more about ourselves. We are accountable to God and not to public opinion.

Compulsive self-preoccupation is not broken by trying to stop thinking about ourselves. That is a self-centered way of trying to be less self-centered. It's like trying not to think about monkeys; the harder you try the more they dance in your mind. We need "the expulsive power of a new affection." Self-forgetfulness begins when we look to Christ, who calls us out of ourselves and into the lives of others.

Prayer: O Lord, save us from self-preoccupation. Give us a healthy self-love and a helpful self-forgetfulness. In Jesus' name. Amen.

Thought: Remembered by God, I can forget myself and think of others.

Week Five, Day Six

Luke 10:25-37
Galatians 5:22

Commanded And Created

Jesus commands us to love: "Love your neighbor as yourself" (Mark 12:31), and "Love one another; even as I have loved you" (John 13:34). Having illustrated love with the story of the good Samaritan, Jesus says, "Go and do likewise" (Luke 10:37). Yet Paul lists love as a "fruit of the Spirit" (Galatians 5:22). Here love is not commanded, but created by the Holy Spirit.

The apparent contradiction is resolved in awareness that love involves both action and attitude. Actions can be commanded. Jesus says in effect, "Here is someone in need; help that person." We need not like the person to obey the command. The test of love in this situation is not our feeling but our action.

Love is also an attitude of compassion and concern. This love is not romantic attraction or even liking someone. It is to care and wish good for another. Such compassionate caring is the fruit of the love-creative Spirit at work within us.

Prayer: O Lord, give us the will to obey and the willingness to be transformed. In his name. Amen.

Thought: I will act as Christ commands and be created as he intends.

The Time To Love

A little girl was asked to give a blood transfusion to save her brother's life. She thought only a moment and then agreed. When the transfusion was completed, she looked up at the nurse and asked, "When do I die?" In everyone's concern for the brother, no one had been aware that she believed that to give her blood was to give her life. In her heart that little girl gave her life for her brother, and in some small measure such is every act of love.

In crisis situations most family members would probably risk their lives for one another. Yet in the daily routines, we often fail to give even our time or attention to those we love. We let preoccupation with the trivial crowd out the vital.

A bumper sticker asks, "Have you hugged your kid today?" Hugging, like all acts of love, is something we can never do yesterday. Now is the time to give a hug, write a letter, make a call, sign a check, say a word, do a deed that gives a little of our life and our love to those for whom we care.

Prayer: O Lord, save us from being only loving in general. Enable us to love specific people here and now. In Jesus' name. Amen.

Thought: Giving life is giving love.

The Great Discovery

There are fleeting pleasures in the self-saving life, but there is also enduring frustration. When caught in a cycle of self-seeking and self-preoccupation, we become increasingly miserable. A voice from within says, "This is not it! This is not the life you were meant to live!" Lincoln could now speak to us as he did to an irritated young man: "My friend, there is something wrong with you on the inside."

The self-losing life has its problems, too. We are not promised perpetual happiness. "If the world hates you," said Jesus, "know that it has hated me before it hated you ... If they persecuted me, they will persecute you" (John 15:18, 20). To love is to be vulnerable. We follow a Christ whose way of living brought him to a cross.

Yet as we venture with him, abandoning ourselves in trust to the love of God and with love to care for people, our inner voice speaks of a great discovery: "This is it! This has the taste and touch of life upon it! This is the life I was meant to live! This is being the person I was born to be!" Following Jesus is not always easy, but it is always the way we are designed to live.

Prayer: O Lord, give us only the problems of living rightly in a sinful world. In Jesus' name. Amen.

Thought: When in tune with Jesus, I am true to myself.

Isaiah 43:1-7
1 Corinthians 6:19, 20

Belonging

What matters most is not who we are, but whose we are. The essential question is not, "What do you do? How much do you earn? What do you own?" or even, "Who are you?" but, "To whom do you belong?"

As we trust his mercy, we belong to God and have a place among his people. In Christ his promise to Israel is for every person: "Fear not, for I have redeemed you; I have called you by name, you are mine ... You are precious in my eyes, and honored, and I love you" (Isaiah 43:1, 4). As we rest in that promise we begin to live in what Karl Barth called "the strange new world within the Bible."

It is strange at first and amazing to the last, but the more we live by the love and power of God, the more we feel at home in his presence. He convicts and corrects us; and yet, like the prodigal come home, we rejoice to be where we belong. "You are not your own," says Paul; "you were bought with a price" (1 Corinthians 6:19, 20). Something in us rebels against that ownership, but something deeper celebrates: "I am his, I am at home!"

Prayer: Say it to me again, Lord, "You are mine ... You are precious ... I love you." Thank you. Amen.

Thought: When I belong to God, I am at home with myself.

The Heart Of Being Human

We may be told, "Be a man!" or "Be a lady!" But can you imagine telling a dog to be a dog or a cat to be a cat? Dogs and cats are what they are, but we humans are not. We live subhuman lives and need to become who we are. But what then is involved in being fully human?

"The entire way of life for the Christian person," said Luther, consists in just two things: "Faith and love ... Faith receives, love gives." Is receiving love and giving love the vital center not just of being Christian, but of being truly human? From Christ, from scripture, and from experience, we answer, "Yes!" We are designed to be loved and to love. Being loved and loving are the alternate beats of the human heart.

We are created "in the image of God" (Genesis 1:27). We are designed to live in God's love and to share that love with others. In Jesus we see that the essence of humanity is in living with openness to receive and to express the divine love. This is central; all else is peripheral. Jesus was both "the man of God" and "the man for others." As he was, so we all are created to be. So, by his grace we can more nearly be!

Prayer: O Lord, bring us back to the basics of living. Give us openness to welcome and to share your love. In Jesus' name. Amen.

Thought: Loved and loving — this is the heart of my humanity.

Philippians 1:3-11
2 Timothy 1:8-14

A Few Certainties

"The older I become the fewer certainties I require." These words from an elderly pastor are increasingly true for me. It is no longer necessary to have a final opinion on every question. We acknowledge the mystery of life and the complexity of issues that pit persons of equal intelligence and virtue against each other. With resources to live from and purposes to live for, we have peace and direction in the midst of uncertainty.

An old professor confessed that in crises times, he turned again to verses learned as a child. "God so loved the world that he gave his only Son" (John 3:16), "Beloved, if God so loved us, we also ought to love one another" (1 John 4:11). These are the certainties confirmed in Christ.

It is told that on a night of many falling stars, some feared that the end had come. Lincoln, however, remained calm, for he looked beyond the meteors to the "grand old constellations that still stood their places." The certainties of Christ, like the constellations, stand firm. We take our bearings not from the falling stars, but from Jesus, and in every situation, we follow him in trust and in love.

Prayer: O Lord, keep us firm at the center and flexible at the periphery. In Jesus' name. Amen.

Thought: Centered on Christ, I am calm in complexity.

Week Six, Day Five

Psalm 84:1-12
Luke 15:11-24

Homecoming

G. K. Chesterton said that "men are homesick in their homes and strangers under the sun and they lay their heads in a foreign land, whenever the day is done." Most of us have sung: "I am but a stranger here, heaven is my home." These lines convey a half-truth. We are pilgrims on the earth and with Abraham look "forward to the city which has foundations, whose builder and maker is God" (Hebrews 11:10). At the same time, this world is our home and it is here we "abide" in the presence of Christ (John 15:4).

Our problem is not that we are aliens from another realm, but that we seek to live a foreign style of life that is contrary to our design. We are homesick not just for heaven someday, but for authentic life now. Something in us is sick of the futility of self-centered living. We long for someone to trust, someone to love, something for which to live.

Yielding to Christ is like homecoming. If God "so loved the world" that he sent his Son to live in it (John 3:16), we can hardly regard this place and its people as foreign. Here we live, are loved, and love.

Prayer: O God, as you love the world, enable us to care for this place and its people. In Jesus' name. Amen.

Thought: Home is everywhere I am with Christ.

This Is My Father's World

Living by grace changes our sense of the world. We are overwhelmed by the privilege of being alive and able to behold the universe. With John Burroughs we say, "The longer I live, the more my mind dwells upon the beauty and wonder of the world." Something in us feels like singing:

This is my Father's world, And to my listening ears
All nature sings, and round me rings The music of
the spheres.

This is my Father's world: I rest me in the thought
Of rocks and trees, of skies and seas; His hand
the wonders wrought.

This is my Father's world, The birds their carols
raise,
The morning light, the lily white, Declare their
Maker's praise.

Someone has said that we shall be called to account for all the permitted pleasure we have failed to enjoy. Our sins of omission include failure to receive the joy God wills for us as well as failure to give the joy he intends for others. "As birds in the morning sing God's praise," our joyous welcome of all things glad and good gives glory to God.

Prayer: O Lord, we bow in awe before the wonder of your world. Thank you for all things beautiful. In Jesus' name. Amen.

Thought: With God as my Father, his world is my home.

Week Six, Day Seven

Psalm 8:1-9
Luke 12:22-34

Two Views Of Self

Imagine two maps: one of your local area, the other of the world. Your community fills the entire local map, but if shown at all, your city is only a tiny dot on the world map.

The place of our community on such maps illustrates two views of ourselves. We can see ourselves as filling the whole map. Nothing else exists beyond us — we are everything. Or we can see ourselves as, at most, a tiny dot so little in comparison to the vastness around us that we count for next to nothing.

In Christ we discover that we need something of each perspective. Each of us is only one among billions on a tiny planet in a universe incomprehensibly vast in time and space. Yet every person is a creature of complexity comparable to the mystery of the physical universe and of worth far greater still. Each of us has a place in the love of God and of people no other can fill. When one says of another, "Nobody can take his place," it is a fact true of us all.

Prayer: O Lord, save us from seeing ourselves as either all or nothing. Show us our little place and our infinite worth. In Jesus' name. Amen.

Thought: I'm only little, but I'm on God's map.

An Unfolding Adventure

Life in grace is paradoxically total, yet always partial; it is final, yet incomplete; once and for all, yet endlessly unfolding.

In Christ, nothing is held back. We are fully forgiven, totally loved, offered the full power of his healing Holy Spirit. In the joy of new life, we yield ourselves in total surrender, withholding nothing. It seems as if we have arrived. Old sins are wiped away, doubt and despair vanish; we are grasped by grace, and gladness bounds.

But there is no guarantee that this rapture will last. Indeed, such mountaintop experiences are sometimes followed by valleys of despair, known to the saints as "dark nights of the soul." Then we know we have not arrived. Old temptations rise as if from the dead. Doubts that had vanished reappear. Even after having sincerely yielded all to Christ, we discover areas held back for ourselves.

Yet like pilgrims, we venture on, assured in Christ that our wavering trust, faltering hope, and listless love do not nullify the endless mercy of God. Each morning begins a new "day full of grace" and a time to begin again.

Prayer: O Lord, whatever the peaks or valleys, give us confidence that you are our companion to the end. In Jesus' name. Amen.

Thought: I have not arrived, but with Christ I am on the way.

Continuous Conversion

E. Stanley Jones believed that "we need to be converted at least once a year on general principles." Oswald Chambers said that "we have to be continuously converted all the days of our lives." It is not enough, nor is it even necessary, to have a dramatic conversion experience. Some, like Paul, are stopped in their tracks and brought suddenly into new life. Yet the days that follow are not all roses. Years later Paul confessed: "We were so utterly, unbearably crushed that we despaired of life itself. Why, we felt that we had received the sentence of death" (2 Corinthians 1:8, 9).

But that was not the end of the story. Those afflictions were an occasion for new yielding and renewed hope: "That was to make us rely not on ourselves but on God who raises the dead; he delivered us from so deadly a peril, and he will deliver us; on him we have set our hope that he will deliver us again" (2 Corinthians 1:9, 10).

Through Peter's denial and restoration, God also assures us that when we fall, he is with us to lift us up. The present is the moment of grace. In this moment we are born again, and again, and again.

Prayer: O Lord, bring us daily out of our old and into your new. In Jesus' name. Amen.

Thought: My trust is not in past experiences, but in present grace.

John 3:1-15
Ephesians 2:1-10

Day After Day

Luther goes beyond urging yearly conversion; he advocates daily resurrection. Luther builds on Paul's statement that "we were buried therefore with him by baptism into death, so that as Christ was raised from the dead by the glory of the Father, we, too, might walk in newness of life" (Romans 6:4). He says that our baptism "means that our sinful self, with all its evil deeds and desires, should be drowned through daily repentance; and that day after day a new self should arise to live with God in righteousness and purity forever."

The daily dying and daily rising is part of the rhythm of joyful living. In daily abandonment to Christ we die to the distortions that make us subhuman and are born again into life-giving grace that enables "newness of life."

Some can date their conversion, others cannot. Some see new birth in the event of their baptism, others in an emotional encounter with the Holy Spirit. But whatever may have been, "now is the day of salvation" (2 Corinthians 6:2). Now is the moment of grace.

Prayer: O Lord, lift us daily from death to newness of life. In Jesus' name. Amen.

Thought: Resurrection each day foretells resurrection someday.

Week Seven, Day Four

Luke 9:18-25
1 Peter 1:3-9

Birth Pangs

Anguish as well as joy often accompanies initial and daily new birth. Paul Sonnack's words ring true to our experience: "We do not learn what dependence on God is except through having our own self-dependence broken in the mill of life, slowly, painfully with many tears and much shame and continual repentance."

We learn, for example, that being forgiven is not the experience of pure joy some think it to be. To be caught in a shameful deed and to have no recourse but to confess and cast ourselves on another's mercy, is at best painfully humiliating. No wonder we flee confession like the plague and create elaborate rationalizations to excuse ourselves.

When confronted with personal sin, our first response is not always to cry with the publican, "God, be merciful to me a sinner" (Luke 18:13), but rather to say with Pilate, "I am innocent" (Matthew 27:24). Even when convicted, we may cry with Peter, "Depart from me, for I am a sinful man" (Luke 5:8). Only after many tears did Peter, following his denial, come through the pain to "rejoice with unutterable and exalted joy" (1 Peter 1:8). So, too, for us, being broken and being born are often painful business.

Prayer: O Christ of the cross and of Easter, bring us through pangs of birth to joys of life. In Jesus' name. Amen.

Thought: Pain and joy are part of being born.

Week Seven, Day Five

Luke 18:9-14
Romans 5:1-11

Saints And Sinners

A saint is a forgiven sinner. As we look to Christ and trust his mercy, we are accepted and welcomed into the embrace of his love. Yet, being loved does not instantly make us better than before. We are simultaneously saints and sinners.

In Christ we are saved *in* our sins. "God shows his love for us in that while we were yet sinners Christ died for us" (Romans 5:8). Our faith falters, our love wanes; and when seemingly most holy, we may in pride be most sinful of all. Christ exposes sins of which we had been unaware. In him we cannot be content to be as good as our friends. The life of Jesus is now the standard of our lives, and before him we have nothing of which to boast. In his mercy is our only hope.

In Christ we are also saved *from* our sins. Jesus is the one who "will save his people from their sins" (Matthew 1:21). In him we are being both loved and healed. He both forgives and cleanses: "If we confess our sins, he ... will forgive our sins and cleanse us from all unrighteousness" (1 John 1:9).

Prayer: O Lord, thank you for loving us as we are. Now by your Spirit, transform us daily toward the likeness of Christ. In his name. Amen.

Thought: "He breaks the power of cancelled sin, he sets the prisoner free."

Week Seven, Day Six

Romans 8:31-39
1 John 3:19-24

Guilty But Forgiven

When we are hurtful of ourselves or others, it is right to feel guilty about it. Pangs of regret reveal that conscience is alive and well. But can we feel guilty and yet be forgiven? Yes! Forgiveness does not remove feelings of regret. Forgiveness assures us that God still loves us. "By this we ... reassure our hearts before him whenever our hearts condemn us; for God is greater than our hearts" (1 John 3:19-20). Luther said that when the devil tells us our sins are too big for God to forgive, we should reply that our real sins are far worse than any he has mentioned and that God knows them all and yet still loves us.

Suppose careless driving takes a life. Feelings of remorse abound. Forgiveness does not remove those guilty feelings, but it does promise that we are still held in the love of God. We may even wish God would hate us as much as we despise ourselves. But God does not hate. He continues to love and bears in his own heart the anguish of our failure and regret. The meeting of that love and our sins raises the cross — on the hill of Calvary and in the suffering heart of God.

Prayer: O Lord, when we are filled with self-loathing, assure us that you still love us and will bring us through. In Jesus' name. Amen.

Thought: My regrets do not cancel God's promises.

Week Seven, Day Seven

Psalm 105:1-6
Acts 3:1-21

The Cycle Of Renewal

The pilgrimage of authentic living is not perpetual victory. There are victories, but seldom from our successful conquest. More often they come through painful surrender of our strength and our weakness to the power of God, who brings triumph out of tragedy and life out of death.

Gerhard Frost used to think the best gifts were on the top shelf and that we had to stretch tall to reach them; now he believes that they are on the bottom shelf and that we must kneel to receive them. For self-made, self-righteous people, kneeling seems repulsive; but for sinners before a holy God it is always in order.

The cycle of renewal starts as we hear promises of God's love, begin to wonder, and then dare to trust that God cares for us. Welcomed as we are, we let go of our pretenses and confess our pride. We abandon our idols and let down defenses against the Spirit. We lose our lives in self-forgetful faith and self-giving love. Now our feet are on the way of joyful living, but it is always a beginning. The cycle continues — grace creates faith, confrontation creates confession, forgiveness creates repentance, love creates life.

Prayer: O God, wherever we are in the venture of living, renew us this day in faith, hope, and love. In Jesus' name. Amen.

Thought: "Our inner nature is being renewed every day" (2 Corinthians 4:16).

Week Eight, Day One

Romans 6:12-23
Galatians 5:1-15

Under New Management

In Christ we are under new management. He is not only our Savior but our Lord, not only "Jesus, lover of my soul" but also "Jesus, Master, whose I am." Something in us does not take kindly to being under the management of anybody or anything. We will rule our own lives and determine our destiny. But such thinking flies in the face of the facts. We are no more God than we are Napoleon. To imagine ourselves either is to be out of touch with reality. We are designed not to be sovereign, but to be servants of Christ.

Here is one of the most profound paradoxes of living. We are, says Paul, "slaves of God" (Romans 6:22). Yet Paul can also say, "For freedom Christ has set us free; stand fast therefore, and do not submit again to a yoke of slavery" (Galatians 5:1). It is strange but true — in surrender to the Lordship of Christ and in yielding to the sovereignty of God, we receive an amazing freedom. It is freedom *from* tyrants that have sought to control and destroy us, freedom *for* new joy and strength in God's service, freedom to fulfill our potential as persons.

Prayer:

Make me a captive, Lord, And then I shall be free ...
My heart is weak and poor Until it master find ...
It cannot freely move Till thou has wrought its chain;
Enslave it with thy matchless love,
And deathless it shall reign. Amen.

Thought: I am created for the love *and the Lordship* of Christ.

Week Eight, Day Two

Deuteronomy 5:6-10
Mark 12:13-17

Our Supreme Allegiance

Yielding to God is the only surrender which does not diminish our humanity. Total surrender to anything else — self, passion, possessions, greed, government, drugs, ambition — degrades and ultimately destroys us. Yielding all to God affirms the creative freedom with which we are designed to live. Yielding all to anyone or anything less than God abdicates our responsibility as persons. God's will is not only our peace, but is also our freedom.

Yielded to God, we surrender to no other. As Christian citizens, for example, we regularly obey the laws of the land, but do not look to Uncle Sam as if he were God. We will never concede to any government that "we will do whatever you say." Such surrender to the will of the state is not patriotism but idolatry. We "render to Caesar the things that are Caesar's, and to God that things that are God's" (Mark 12:17). But we always remember that our conscience and our supreme allegiance belong not to Caesar, not to any human authority, but to God alone.

Prayer: O Lord, we surrender to you and ask for courage to stand firm against all who bid for our total allegiance. Save us from every form of idolatry and give us instead the faith to let you be God alone. In Jesus' name. Amen.

Thought: I stand with Peter and the Apostles saying, "We must obey God rather than any human authority" (Acts 5:29 NRSV).

Week Eight, Day Three 2 Corinthians 5:11-21
Romans 8:18-25

Controlled By Love

Paul was no puppet. He was free and responsible — deciding, acting, writing, witnessing, always moving forward with the vigor of personal initiative. Yet Paul says, "The love of Christ controls us" (2 Corinthians 5:14). In Paul we see that the control of Christ liberates us for full assertion of our human powers.

Love does not stifle; it enhances and enables. If a human "love" is undermining our creativity and suffocating our capacity for growth, it is doubtful that it is really love at all. True love brings out the best that is in us.

So also with the perfect love of God in Christ. When we let his love control us we are set free to live in what Paul calls "the glorious liberty of the children of God" (Romans 8:21). When captive to our own passions and desires, we are like a caged bird; we are limited by the confines of our own self-interest. Controlled by the love of Christ, we are freed to fly in a new world as wide and as high as the care of Christ. His love now sets the limits, and those are vaster by far than any of our own creating.

Prayer: O Christ, we yield our lives to your control. Free us from the constraints of self-centeredness and give us the liberty of your love. In your name. Amen.

Thought: Controlled by love, I am free to live.

John 8:31-38
Hebrews 12:3-11

Free Indeed

We continue to ponder the paradox of being controlled by Christ and yet free to be fully ourselves. To illustrate, imagine two athletes: one lives under the strict discipline of a wise and caring coach; the other lives an easy life of self-indulgence. The first carries out a vigorous program of exercise, practice, and diet. The second follows only the impulses of the moment and is sporadic in practice, lazy in exercise, careless about diet. Now comes the day of the great race. The question is not, "Who will win?" but "Who is free to fulfill his or her potential as a person?" Only the first has freedom for that.

To win the race or to achieve wealth or fame while living far short of our potential is to have failed as a person. The control of Christ, like the discipline of a wise and caring coach, limits our impulses to self-indulgence, while at the same time liberating us to fulfill our humanity. As the control of the coach and the initiative of the athlete complement each other, so also there is no contradiction between the control of Christ and personal initiative toward wholeness. Yielded to his love, we are free to live, to love, to grow. In Christ we are "free indeed!" (John 8:36).

Prayer: O Lord, give us wisdom to obey your coaching. Discipline us into the freedom of fullness of life. In your name. Amen.

Thought: Christ limits me only to fulfill me.

 2 Corinthians 12:1-10
Romans 8:28-39

God Works For Good

With Jesus as Lord we expect victory over every evil. Sometimes this means immediate release from an oppressive affliction. By the healing touch of God's Spirit, sickness is healed, fear removed, and temptation shattered with such suddenness that we are stunned with grateful amazement.

But it is not always so. When Paul prayed for deliverance from his thorn in the flesh, the answer was not immediate healing, but assurance that "my grace is sufficient for you, for my power is made perfect in weakness" (2 Corinthians 12:8, 9). The affliction remained, but its power was broken. The oppression became an occasion for revelation. God used "a messenger of Satan" (2 Corinthians 12:7) to reveal his grace.

The affliction was not a blessing. It remained evil, but God used it for good. "In everything" — and that means *everything*: good, bad, and indifferent — "God works for good with those who love him" (Romans 8:28). He heals, delivers, and gives strength to endure; but more — he uses evil for good. The way to victory is through surrender — not to evil, but of evil to God.

Prayer: O Lord, let no evil have dominion over us. Give us the confidence of your children. In Jesus' name. Amen.

Thought: In God's mill, even evil is grist for good.

Week Eight, Day Six

1 Corinthians 4:1-5
1 Peter 4:7-11

Trustees

As we trust in God, he is also trusting in us. Under Christ, we are managers of all that he gives us. "This is how one should regard us," says Paul, "as servants of Christ and stewards of the mysteries of God. Moreover it is required of stewards that they be found trustworthy" (1 Corinthians 4:1, 2).

We are stewards whether we like it or believe it or not. God has entrusted us with life and the gifts of life, including all the resources of the earth. We may be faithful or not, but the fact remains — we are trustees responsible to God.

For a factory manager to run the business at his own pleasure and for his own profit would be blatant theft. So also, when we regard God's gifts as ours, we are in effect stealing from him. Responsible stewardship is not a matter of giving generously of what we have stolen from God. It is rather the faithful management of all he has entrusted to us. Then our giving is a sign of our stewardship and not just a substitute for it.

Prayer: O Lord, deepen our sense of the "giftness" of life; enable us to be trustworthy managers of all your blessings. In Jesus' name. Amen.

Thought: "All that we have is thine alone, a trust, O Lord, from thee."

Week Eight, Day Seven

Genesis 39:1-9
1 Corinthians 9:15-27

Under Higher Orders

A social worker battling frustration and failure with hardcore addicts was asked, "How do you keep going?" She replied, "I guess it's because I am under higher orders. I don't have to succeed, but I do have to keep trying." Such is our situation under the Lordship of Christ.

These are his orders for today: "A new commandment I give to you, that you love one another; even as I have loved you" (John 13:34). "Go therefore and make disciples of all nations" (Matthew 28:19).

With the orders come these promises: "I am with you always, to the close of the age" (Matthew 28:20). "You shall receive power when the Holy Spirit has come upon you" (Acts 1:8).

Mindful of higher orders, and sustained by Christ's promises, we do not give up. We may not succeed, but we keep working and witnessing. "Having this ministry by the mercy of God, we do not lose heart" (2 Corinthians 4:1). This is his promise: "In the Lord your labor is not in vain" (1 Corinthians 15:58).

Prayer: O Lord, give us strength to persevere in your service. In Jesus' name. Amen.

Thought: This is my motto for living: "My utmost for his highest."

Week Nine, Day One

John 14:12-31
Acts 1:1-8

Life In The Spirit

Love is not enough. We also need power — life-lifting, life-enabling power. In God the Holy Spirit, that power is with us. The Holy Spirit is God himself, present and powerful, willing and working to enable our wholeness.

The biblical message of grace, as Reinhold Niebuhr stressed, promises both the mercy of God toward us and the power of God at work with us and within us. In that mercy, seen supremely in Jesus Christ, we are welcomed every moment. By that power, offered in the life-giving Holy Spirit, we live with nothing less than the possibilities of the presence of God.

Having been given the great commission, the disciples did not rush off to fulfill it. They remembered the promise, "You shall receive power when the Holy Spirit has come upon you" (Acts 1:8). They waited together — prayerful, open, receptive. Then came Pentecost and experience of the Spirit. Now the new community in Christ was assured of strength supplied by the presence of God. That same power now waits, wills, and works to bless and use us.

Prayer: Holy Spirit of God, be for us now the most intimate and most mighty presence in our lives. In Jesus' name. Amen.

Thought: God with and God within, God of love and God of power — this is the Holy Spirit.

Week Nine, Day Two

John 20:19-23
1 Corinthians 12:4-31

Receive The Holy Spirit

> *Jesus said to them again, "Peace be with you. As the Father has sent me, even so I send you." And when he had said this, he breathed on them, and said to them, "Receive the Holy Spirit."*
>
> — John 20:21, 22

That word of peace and power is for you and for me. We are invited — indeed commanded — to "receive the Holy Spirit."

Jesus did not say, "*Achieve* the Holy Spirit." We need not work ourselves into a frenzy in order to capture the Divine Presence. God is with us now wishing to enter our lives. As we pray, "Holy Spirit, enter in," we move on at once to pray, "Thank you, Lord, for being now at work within my life."

But what are the signs of the Spirit's presence? Some find blessing in such gifts as speaking in tongues or healing and rightly thank God for them, but we are wary of regarding these as the only, or even the most important manifestations of the Spirit. The "gifts" of the Spirit (1 Corinthians 12:4-31) are neither intended for nor needed by everyone. The "fruit of the Spirit" qualities (Galatians 5:22) are for all. These are the universal characteristics of Christ-likeness.

Prayer: Spirit of God, fill us with your presence; heal us by your power. In Jesus' name. Amen.

Thought: I need not work to bring in the Spirit. It takes work to keep him out!

Week Nine, Day Three

Galatians 5:16-26
Ephesians 4:11-16

Attributes Of Authentic Living

How many of the following do you wish were more abundant in your life and the lives of others: "love, joy, peace, patience, kindness, goodness, faithfulness, gentleness, self-control"? (Galatians 5:22). We answer together, "We want them all!"

These qualities picture the person each of us would like to be. They also picture Jesus, in whose life we see them all. In him, we see what it is to be fully human. These qualities, then, are among the central attributes of authentic living.

Note that they are "the fruit *of the Spirit*" and not "the fruit of our striving." Other texts tell us to love; to rejoice; to live at peace; to be patient, kind, good, faithful, gentle, and self-controlled. But, as we will and work to live this life, we do so with confidence that God is willing and working to enable us to do so. Here we pray, "Thy will *and* mine be done." Like yielding to the doctor who wills our health, abandon to God, who wills our wholeness, affirms and fulfills our yearning to be fully human.

Prayer: Life-giving Spirit, make us fruitful in everything from love to self-control. In Jesus' name. Amen.

Thought: I want to grow; God wills my growth.

Week Nine, Day Four

2 Timothy 1:1-7
1 John 4:13-21

From Love To Self-Control

In Paul's list of the "fruit of the Spirit" (Galatians 5:22) love comes first. To love is to give ourselves. We love God by giving ourselves to him in the abandonment of receptive trust. We let him love us, and then "we love, because he first loved us" (1 John 4:19).

Self-control comes last, as the result not of self-centered discipline, but of self-giving surrender. It is the consequence, not the precondition, of a life yielded to the Spirit. "Abandon to the love of Christ," says Chambers, "is the one thing that bears fruit."

Jess Lair says that we love others by telling what is in "our deepest heart." Paul Tournier believes that we give more help by sharing our defeats than our victories. Honest confession of weakness is part of self-giving love. Through confession of limited control of temper and temptation, we yield to the Spirit, who gives growth in self-control. When "the love of Christ controls us" (2 Corinthians 5:14), we can begin to control ourselves.

Prayer: O Lord, help us to begin with being loved and being loving, and then by your power to grow in self-control. In Jesus' name. Amen.

Thought: Self-control follows Christ-control.

Week Nine, Day Five

2 Kings 5:1-14
John 5:1-9

Victory Through Surrender

How are we changed? Self-effort makes a difference. We make resolutions and carry some out. But such success is usually in superficial matters. Deep changes in our patterns of life do not come so easily. Willpower alone cannot overcome the powerful temptations, compulsions, obsessions, and phobias that often plague our lives.

Think, for example, of the sincere alcoholic who has resolved 1,000 times to control his drinking but to no avail. Then he hears the promise of new life in Alcoholics Anonymous and begins to live the program. He abandons self-effort and comes "to believe in a Power greater than ourselves" that can "restore us to sanity." Will and life are turned over "to the care of God," and, with such surrender, victory begins.

All who have visited with joyful recovered alcoholics see such surrender, not as diminishing, but as affirming and fulfilling their humanity. Dependence on alcohol degrades personhood. Dependence on God exalts us and enables fulfillment of our potential as persons. To be helpless is not to be hopeless. In many struggles, the way to victory is through surrender.

Prayer: Life-giving Spirit, we surrender our weakness and receive your strength. In our helplessness, be our hope. In Jesus' name. Amen.

Thought: "Our extremities are God's opportunities."

Week Nine, Day Six

Romans 5:20–6:4
2 Timothy 1:8-14

We Can't, But God Can

He spoke of the burden of many troubles and of promises that invite us to "take them to the Lord, and leave them there." "But," he said, "I can't let go. I try, believe me, I try, but I cannot."

But we do not surrender by trying. So long as we try, we are still fighting. As Paul Tillich says of being "struck by grace": "It happens; or it does not happen. And certainly it does *not* happen when we try to force it upon ourselves, just as it shall not happen so long as we think, in our self-complacency, that we have no need of it." Yet, as we sense our need, and cease trying to force it upon ourselves, it does happen.

When we struggle, Jesus says: "Set your troubled hearts at rest. Trust in God always; trust also in me" (John 14:1 NEB). In Christ we even surrender our inability to surrender. At times we can only confess: "O God, I can't surrender, I can't trust you. I can't do anything. It's all up to you." God answers such prayers. Enabled by his grace, we cease to struggle and discover that surrender has happened without our striving.

Prayer: O Lord, lift from us the burdens from which we cannot free ourselves. Thank you. In Jesus' name. Amen.

Thought: I can't, but God can. Thanks be to God!

Week Nine, Day Seven

John 14:8-17
Ephesians 3:14-21

Ponder The Possibilities

Ponder the possibilities of the self-centered versus the Spirit-centered life. When centered in self, we are like a sailor who looks only at the sea around him. The waves beat against the ship but give no sense of direction. When centered in the Spirit, we are like a sailor who takes his bearings from the stars. We look to Christ and are assured that though we are in a sea of troubles the greater reality is God with us.

We are finite, weak, confused, and sinful. Sickness and death dog our days. But so what! God is with us! He has given each of us enough ability to do his will. His Spirit moves with a healing touch in the darkest corners of our sinful hearts and troubled minds. No area even of our subconscious is beyond the reach of his healing power. No burden is too heavy for him to lift and bear.

We are not able, but we are enabled to face each day with quiet confidence and steady hope. We are weak, but God is strong. He is "able to do far more abundantly than all that we ask or think" (Ephesians 3:20). Whatever our problems, the possibilities of his presence open before us.

Prayer: O Lord, when we are unable to trust or to care, enable us again to live with faith and love. In Jesus' name. Amen.

Thought: My problems fade before God's possibilities.

1 Thessalonians 5:9-24
Hebrews 10:19-25

We Need One Another

Karl Barth said that "ein Mensch ist kein Mensch" (one person is not a person). John Brantner says that we discover our wholeness through encounter with others. Lives cut off from human love and loving are less than fully human.

Solitude and togetherness are both vital to joyful living. We need times and places to be alone, to rest and reflect, to ponder and to pray. We also need one another and are made more human by every relationship of love and caring.

Some relationships hurt more than help. We live better alone than with some people. No community is totally positive in its influence upon us. Indeed, our greedy, competitive, materialistic culture may be more dehumanizing than most of us realize. We are designed not to be parts of an economic machine, but to be persons in a sustaining community of caring people. A cousin said of our mother at her death: "She always encouraged me." We pray that our lives, too, will be an encouragement to others, and a force for a more humane social order.

Prayer: Thank you, Lord, for everyone who adds meaning to our lives. Enable us to be such persons to others. In Jesus' name. Amen.

Thought: Those who love me help to create me.

Week Ten, Day Two

Luke 10:25-37
Philippians 1:1-11

Our Most Important People

Who are the most important in your world? If your list is like mine, it includes two groups: (1) those I need, and (2) those who need me. Some people are on both lists.

Among our most needed are those who nourish us with personal care and concern. Their affection is food and drink for our fullness of life. Even if only one or two really care for us, we have a blessing for which to be deeply grateful. Each of us has probably received more love than we realize. Without it we could not have survived this well this long. Those who give the love we need are certainly among our most important people.

But there are also the equally important people who need us. Our caring for them is as essential to our welfare as to theirs. We cannot ignore the needs of others and continue to be fully human. To live without self-giving love is to forsake our highest nature and, in the long run, to lose the meaning and joy of life itself. To live with love is to be both lively and life-giving.

Prayer: O Lord, give us courage to be both the cared for and the caring. In Jesus' name. Amen.

Thought: The needed and the needy are my most important people.

Week Ten, Day Three

Matthew 7:7-12
Luke 6:27-38

Sponges?

We may dislike being compared to sponges, but there is a sense in which each of us is to be a sponge, soaking up all the love and wisdom God and people pour upon us. We seek to learn and to receive from every person we meet. This receiving, while enriching us, does not impoverish them. They, too, are blessed in their giving.

Then, having received, we are to give. Having soaked up so much, we are, in effect, to wring ourselves out for others. Such soaking up and wringing out is another picture of the cycle of receiving and giving that is at the heart of joyful living.

The Sea of Galilee receives and gives and thus lives and is life-giving. The Dead Sea, which has no outlet, only receives but does not give and so is dead. Getting without giving is deadly business, and not least financially. Our money has been likened to manure — piled up it is useless and repulsive, spread on the fields it is life-giving. Is this illustration offensive? Perhaps, but no more than the greedy hoarding of blessings intended for the good of others. "I never had any fun with my money," said one millionaire, "until I began to do good with it."

Prayer: O Lord, as we freely receive, give us compassion and courage to freely give. In Jesus' name. Amen.

Thought: I will be a sponge, soaking up and wringing out.

Week Ten, Day Four

Luke 9:23-27
Philippians 2:1-11

Find Someone Who Needs You

A psychiatrist gave this prescription: "Find a person or cause that needs you and give yourself in meeting that need." That's wisdom — the happiest people care for the happiness of others.

This does not suggest that we use calculated self-giving to gain self-fulfillment. Such is only another form of greedy self-saving. Jesus's words, "Those who want to save their life will lose it, and those who lose their life for my sake will save it" (Luke 9:24 NRSV), are a description of reality, not a prescription for easy, successful living. This is Jesus' prescription: "If any want to be my followers, let them deny themselves and take up their cross daily and follow me" (Luke 9:23 NRSV).

Helping others selfishly is far better than hurting them selfishly, but such calculated "self-losing" is not the way of Christ. If this seems a dilemma, there is a way out — to forget about self-fulfillment and to get busy meeting a real need. When we do that, the joyful living will take care of itself.

Prayer: O Lord, show us the people who need us and give us the willingness and strength to really care for them. In Jesus' name. Amen.

Thought: Self-fulfillment is a by-product of self-forgetful self-giving.

Mark 2:23-27
Luke 12:13-21

The Corporate Dimension

Our task is to care for individuals and also to help create a more human community. The question is not just whether people somewhere can be Christian in a pagan culture, but whether we ourselves can be authentically human while being bombarded by the dehumanizing pressures with which we live.

Life-enhancing qualities abound within our society. We have amazing freedom and abounding opportunities. Millions affirm equal opportunity for all, and agree that "one's life does not consist in the abundance of possessions" (Luke 12:15 NRSV). But how many live out these principles in daily action? How many agree with E. F. Schumacher that "small is beautiful," or see that aspects of our way of life may stifle the creativity, generosity, and cooperative spirit which are essential to true humanity?

The structures of society may seem beyond our influence, but they are not entirely so. We can't change everything, but we can do something. Our voice, vote, and example promote systems in which people matter.

Prayer: Use us, Lord, to help make this world a better place in which to live. In Jesus' name. Amen.

Thought: The systems are made for people, not people for the systems.

Week Ten, Day Six 1 Corinthians 12:12-27
Galatians 6:1-5

A Caring Community

We all need the encouragement of a caring community. For most of us, this care comes through the fellowship of a Christian congregation in which the love of people reflects the love of God. As we worship, study, share, and serve together we are called out of ourselves into a larger family.

There is a place for each of us. None need feel self-rejection. "If the foot should say, 'Because I am not a hand, I do not belong to the body,' that would not make it any less a part of the body" (1 Corinthians 12:15). Nor is there rejection of others. "The eye cannot say to the hand, 'I have no need of you' " (1 Corinthians 12:21). One fact is true for all: "You are the body of Christ and individually members of it" (1 Corinthians 12:2). Or, as E. Stanley Jones liked to say, "Every person who belongs to Christ, belongs to every person who belongs to Christ."

Beyond the group, it helps to have one person with whom we can be open about everything. A friend, family member, pastor, or counselor often helps by only hearing. The saying is true: "When we share our joys, we double them; when we share our troubles, we cut them in half."

Prayer: Thank you, Lord, for a place to belong and for a circle of caring people. In Jesus' name. Amen.

Thought: I belong to the body, and the body belongs to me.

Week Ten, Day Seven

John 3:16, 17
Matthew 19:13-22

Our Circle Of Concern

In Christ our circle of concern is enlarged to include everyone God loves. "I am involved in mankind," said John Donne. "Any man's death diminishes me." As we are diminished by another's death, we are enlarged by others' lives and they by ours.

But how can we love so many? (1) Our caring attitudes are nonverbal, intercessory prayers. We can follow John Brantner's habit of looking at strangers and silently wishing them well. (2) By conserving the limited resources of earth, we care for those who live with us and after us. (3) Our gifts of money are, as Fosdick said, "our time and talent in portable form" going to work for us in places we can't visit personally. (4) Through work for justice we influence governmental decisions that may affect millions.

Christ and human need call us both to help the afflicted and to remove the affliction. As curative and preventive medicine are essential to total health care, deeds of charity and acts for justice are both vital to total human care. Meddling in politics is the business of every caring person.

Prayer: O Lord, deepen our sense of interdependence, and enable us to live in ways that give hope to others. In Jesus' name. Amen.

Thought: I care for all for whom Christ cares.

Week Eleven, Day One

1 Corinthians 1:1-9
Hebrews 10:19-25

Life In Our Larger Families

Many now live in one-person families. Others consist of one parent and one or more children, and others of a couple with children. Some live in extended families with grandparents, aunts and uncles, and other relatives.

This week we will focus more specifically on our larger families beginning with our families of faith, and then on our place within the human family.

I have been involved in Christian congregations all my life and must confess to sometimes having been less than thrilled and inspired by the experience.

At the same time, I must also confess to being increasingly grateful for the privilege of being part of a community that seeks to learn from and to follow Jesus. On most Sundays I am now not in the pulpit but in the pew, and when I look around at the congregation, join in the hymns, hear the scripture readings and sermon, and join in the sacrament of Holy Communion, I am often deeply moved with gratitude for the privilege of being with these people in this place. When I was presiding at worship, I was usually too distracted by what I needed to say and do to think much about that privilege, but I certainly think of it now, and wish for every reader a similar experience within a Christ-centered community.

Prayer: Dear Lord, thank you for good times with your people and for the privilege of listening, learning, growing, and serving together. In your name. Amen.

Thought: Ordinary and sinful as we are, I treasure my congregational family.

We Are One Family In Christ

Each of our faith families is much larger than our local congregation. We also hold family membership in our denomination and in the global family of those who look to Jesus for life and salvation.

Structurally, theologically, liturgically, racially, and in many other ways, this worldwide family is one of the most splintered. Our history to the present day abounds in controversy and conflict. At the same time, we confess to being profoundly united in Christ.

I believe that John Wesley got it right when he said, "Difference in opinion or modes of worship may prevent an entire external union; yet need it prevent our union in affection? Though we cannot think alike, may we not love alike? May we not be of one heart, though we are not of one opinion? Without all doubt we may." With this understanding, Wesley invited everyone who trusted God's promises in Christ to "give me your hand."

Ponder again Stanley Jones' statement, "Every person who belongs to Christ, belongs to every person who belongs to Christ." Whatever our differences, we all look to Christ for life and salvation. United at heart we also rightly say to one another, "Give me your hand."

Prayer: Dear Lord, remind us day by day that as we belong to you, we also belong to all who are part of your family. As we confess our unity, teach us respectfully to affirm our diversity. In your name. Amen.

Thought: Christian unity is not in uniformity but in Christ.

Week Eleven, Day Three

Luke 18:9-14
Acts 13:42-43

Kinship Beyond The Church

Those of us who believe that we are "saved by grace through faith" (Ephesians 2:8) are compelled to ask, "Can God be gracious to those who do not confess Christ?" and "Can such persons be 'saved by grace through faith?' " The texts noted above suggest that the answer to these questions is "Yes." Jesus said of the Jewish sinner who cast himself on the gracious mercy of God that he went home "justified" (Luke 18:14), and at the close of their meeting with Jews and converts to Judaism, Paul and Barnabas "urged them to continue in the grace of God" (Acts 13:43).

These texts remind us that none is saved by our religious affiliation or condemned because of it. We are saved by the grace of God! Although supremely revealed in Jesus, that grace is not solely directed at, nor possessed by, Christians. I believe that Bible verses such as "No one comes to the Father except through me" (John 14:6) and "There is salvation in no one else ..." (Acts 4:12) do not mean that salvation requires correct beliefs concerning Jesus, but that we are saved only by the grace revealed and promised in Jesus. It is as Jesus says, "Whoever believes in me believes not in me but in the one who sent me. And whoever sees me sees him who sent me" (John 12:44-45).

Prayer: Dear God, ground me in your saving grace and empower me to proclaim it to everyone everywhere and to rejoice in all in whom I find it. In Jesus' name. Amen.

Thought: Every person who lives by grace belongs to every person who lives by grace.

The Biggest Family On Earth

Beyond our families of grace and faith, we also belong to the human family and here, too, make another Christian affirmation: "Every person loved by God belongs to every person loved by God!" None of us has ever met or will ever meet a person whom God does not love!

John 3:16 doesn't say that "God so loved the church" or "the Christians." It says, "God so loved the *world*"! That means not only that God loves everyone everywhere, but also that in the love of God every person on this planet is my brother or sister including even those who deny or despise the love of God. We may not like some of them. Some may be our enemies, but with Christ we are to love them all.

Six-year-old Mattie J. T. Stepanek wrote this little poem that might have been titled "Life in the Love of God."

We are growing up. We are many colors of skin.
We are many languages. We are many ages and sizes.
We are many countries ... But we are one earth.
We each have one heart. We each have one life.
We are growing up, together.
So we must each join our Hearts and lives together
And live as one family.

Prayer: Dear God, inspire and enable us to live as befits brothers and sisters in the human family, and as citizens not only of one country but of one world. In Jesus' name. Amen.

Thought: Whenever I meet anyone, anywhere I will try to remember that I am meeting a brother or sister in the love of God whom I also am to love.

Week Eleven, Day Five

Acts 2:43-47; 4:32-35
2 Corinthians 9:6-15

Family Stewardship

In our little families we usually share our time, attention, and money equally or in response to a special need. A child with a chronic illness, for example, will rightly receive far more than a sibling who is healthy. The money in the bank and the food on the table belong to the family and not just to the money-makers and breadwinners.

Imagine what would happen in our family if Carol placed the Thanksgiving turkey before me and I prayed a pious prayer thanking God for giving me the turkey and then proceeded to eat it all by myself. None of us would do that in our little families, but don't we often do it in our larger families? In *The Biblical Vision of Sabbath Economics*, Ched Myers tells us that "today the wealthiest twenty percent of the world's population receives almost 83 percent of the world's income while the poorest twenty percent receive less than two percent!" Those percentages are a powerful indictment of humanity's failure to practice family stewardship.

Most of us have substituted charity and "share our surplus" for the kind of stewardship that recognizes that we are trustees of everything and owners of nothing, and that we are to manage it all for the greatest good of all of our families, including the human family.

Prayer: O Lord, lead me beyond charity to stewardship and commitment to justice for all of my brothers and sisters. In Jesus' name. Amen.

Thought: What right do I have to luxuries for myself while others in the family lack the necessities of life?

Week Eleven, Day Six Matthew 18:15-17; 26:51-56
Luke 22:47-51

Family Conflict Resolution, Part 1

Almost all family conflicts are settled nonviolently, usually by conversation, often by negotiation, sometimes by arbitration and litigation, and if all these fail by separation. The preferred method suggested by Matthew 18 is face-to-face in private conversation. If that fails, we are to try a semiprivate consultation involving only a couple more people. If that doesn't work, we are to seek the wisdom and help of the wider community. Only if that fails are we to separate from one another.

Nothing in the New Testament affirms violent means of solving problems. In the texts noted above Jesus specifically rejects violence and says of use of the sword, "No more of this!" We follow this teaching at almost all levels of family life. Those who attempt to solve their problems by killing people in their homes, communities, and within national boundaries are criminals, but on the level of the international global family many still regard violence and war as legitimate means of conflict resolution. But is global violence really more moral than local violence?

Since we are citizens of the world, all war is civil war. Since we are brothers and sisters in God's love, all war is fratricide. Tragic exceptional circumstances may justify the taking of life, but to affirm abortion, capital punishment, mercy killing, and war as acceptable, institutionalized means of conflict resolution strikes me as contrary to clear teaching and example of Jesus.

Prayer: Empower us, Lord, to be faithful to the way of Christ at every level of family life. In Jesus' name. Amen.

Thought: I will ponder the conviction of Franz Kafka that resorting to violence and war is "a monstrous failure of imagination."

Family Conflict Resolution, Part 2

Every civilized country in the world has created laws, courts, and limited, responsible police power to deal with conflicts. But on the international level of the planetary family, we are largely still stuck at the stage of the legendary "Wild West" where the biggest and fastest gun ruled.

Global family problems require global means of conflict resolution. The United Nations and World Court are significant steps in the right direction, but if the human family is to survive and thrive, we will need to create a global security system that is strong enough to preserve the peace while sufficiently limited so that it does not become a source of tyranny. This will be extremely difficult, but the survival of civilization and even of the human race may depend upon it.

Had such a system been operational when terrorists struck the U.S., truly international resources would have been available to deal with terrorism as a planetary problem. Such terrorist acts should be seen not as war against the United States but as crimes against humanity to be dealt with under international law by an international criminal court, international police forces, and global efforts to eradicate the root causes of terrorism. When such a global security system has been created, the nations of the world will be able to say, as did the Ephesian town clerk, "The courts are open ... bring charges there against one another" (Acts 19:38).

Prayer: Dear Lord, teach us to do globally what every civilized city, state, and nation has learned to do locally: to resolve conflicts through law, courts, and police power instead of violence and war. In Jesus' name. Amen.

Thought: The institution of war-making will be abolished either before or after the next world war.

Love Gives Life

How can we know what is loving and what is not? In complex situations we can't always be sure. But this guideline is helpful: Love gives life! That which most enables and ennobles life is the most loving. Love, like God, is on the side of life.

"Love," says Paul, "does no wrong to a neighbor; therefore love is the fulfilling of the law" (Romans 13:8, 10). Love is the opposite of sin. Sin is anti-life. It is sand in the gears of life. "Sin," as E. Stanley Jones put it, "is not just bad, it is bad for us and bad for everybody." Love is good for us and good for everybody.

We affirm the goodness of life and dedicate ourselves to its preservation and fulfillment. This pro-life principle is the basic moral guideline that shapes all our behavior. We support everything (such as medicine, education, and the arts) that enables and enriches life and oppose everything (such as sickness, hunger, discrimination, and violence) that degrades and destroys life.

Prayer: O Lord, heal us of every life-degrading attitude and action and strengthen everything that enables life for others. In Jesus' name. Amen.

Thought: To act for life is to live with love.

Week Twelve, Day Two

Exodus 20:13
Matthew 26:47-52

Issues Of Life And Death

Affirming life as good, we stand in basic opposition to capital punishment, suicide, abortion, war, and mercy killing. But in tragic circumstances it may be necessary to take one life to preserve another. One might, for example, be compelled to kill someone to stop him from killing others.

There are awesome decisions which life-affirming persons can never make lightly. Life can be taken only in extreme circumstances of tragic necessity and then only when one is clearly compelled to do so for the greater good of others. This approach rejects all easy destruction of life and gives strong support for everything (such as contraception, conservation of vital resources, increased food production, international negotiations for peace) that helps eliminate consideration of killing. It affirms the right to refuse to kill and denies the absolute right of any person to take the life of another. Although situations may compel us to think and to do the unthinkable, we always seek choices that affirm the goodness of life and dedicate ourselves to stand with Christ, who "came that they may have life, and have it abundantly" (John 10:10).

Prayer: O Lord, in the dilemmas of life, give us courage to act with love and wisdom. In Jesus' name. Amen.

Thought: In all my choosing, I choose life!

Week Twelve, Day Three

Exodus 20:1-17
John 13:12-15, 34, 35

The Diamond Rule

The Ten Commandments are God's gift for our good. When interpreted positively, they reveal our essential responsibilities to God and people.

The Golden Rule (Matthew 7:12) is also God's gift for our good. We stand in another's shoes, and ask, "If I were in this situation how would I wish to be treated?" From intimate friendship to issues of international relations, the practice of this rule opens the way to reconciliation.

There is a still higher rule. Jesus teaches us not only to treat others as we wish to be treated, but to "love one another; even as I have loved you" (John 13:34). This is the Diamond Rule, and there is none higher.

There are exceptions to the Golden Rule. The masochist who enjoys suffering should not inflict it on others. There are no exceptions to the Diamond Rule. Christ-like love is never out of order. To ask, "What would Jesus do?" does not solve all ethical dilemmas. He surprised his contemporaries and would surely surprise us. But seeing every dilemma in the light of Christ-like love helps us to act with care and compassion.

Prayer: O Lord, as we experience your love, enable us to express it in our care for others. In your name. Amen.

Thought: My standard is not just in letters, but in a life — the life of Jesus!

Week Twelve, Day Four

Proverbs 16:16-25
Luke 14:28-33

Consider The Consequences

We, and others, reap what we sow. We are free to choose, but not to choose the consequences of our choosing. Having stepped off a cliff, we are not free to stop falling. We therefore ponder the consequences of contemplated action and ask, "Will this deed be helpful to myself and others? How will I feel about it tomorrow? Next year? Will others remember this act with gratitude?"

Imagining the probable consequences of our decisions helps us see them in perspective and be more objective in our choosing. Short-term delight leading to long-term misery is no bargain. Short-term distress contributing to lifelong joy is little sacrifice. In the long run the right thing is always the smart thing. Sin is not only shameful but foolish; goodness is not only good but wise.

All this is as true of community and national decisions as of personal choices. Policies that benefit us now may spell disaster for our grandchildren. It's been said that "a politician thinks of the next election; a statesman of the next generation." In Christ, we live today so that others may have life tomorrow.

Prayer: O Lord, give us strength to endure short-term pain that leads to long-term joy. In Jesus' name. Amen.

Thought: I choose today in light of consequences tomorrow.

Week Twelve, Day Five | 2 Chronicles 10:1-19
Proverbs 1:8, 9; 15:22

A Wider Perspective

In wise decision-making we also consider the judgment of others. Can we share our plan of action with those we most respect? They should not decide for us, but it is often helpful to imagine how they would react, and sometimes it is best to discuss an agonizing dilemma with a trusted friend or counselor who can help us to see things we had failed to consider. If something can't be shared, is it because it is so good that it had best be kept secret, or because it is so bad it can't stand the light of day?

We also ask, "Would the world be better if all were to act this way?" A little dishonesty or cheating may seem harmless, but what if everyone did it? The structure of community built on trust would collapse. If it wouldn't be good for all, it's likely wrong for us. If it's good for all, it's likely right for us.

Again these realities relate to community and nation. Norman Cousins likened the arms race to persons competing to drill the biggest hole in our common boat, and saw atomic war as being waged not just against our enemy, but "against the whole of which we are a part." These are complex matters, but we must ask not only, "What's best for *my* country?" but also, "What is best for *our* world?"

Prayer: O Lord, give us openness to listen and wisdom to act for a stronger society. In Jesus' name. Amen.

Thought: Others help me to be helpful to others.

Week Twelve, Day Six

1 Samuel 18:6-11
Matthew 5:1-12

Too Unhappy To Be Kind?

We often know the good but lack the will and strength to do it. Might we, for example, be among those A. E. Housman called "too unhappy to be kind"?

> *... these are not in plight to bear*
> *If they would, another's care.*
> *They have enough as 'tis: I see*
> *In many an eye that measures me*
> *The mortal sickness of a mind*
> *Too unhappy to be kind.*
> *Undone with misery, all they can*
> *Is to hate their fellow man;*
> *And till they drop they needs must still*
> *look at you and wish you ill.*

Happy people are also unkind, but there is truth in Housman's lines — misery often leads to meanness.

"Happy are the kind-hearted" (Matthew 5:7 Phillips). That says happiness comes from being kind. But the reverse is also true — kindness comes from being happy. As we trust in the love of God and find our joy in him, and in life together with his people, we experience a happiness that helps us to be kind. With thankful joy we now look at others and wish them well.

Prayer: Spirit of Christ, save us from miseries that make us mean. Give us joy enough to act with love. In Jesus' name. Amen.

Thought: Kindness makes me happy; happiness helps me to be kind.

Luke 18:9-14
Romans 8:28

In The Context Of Grace

At best we will make many wrong decisions. The most careful choice may turn out to be a tragic mistake. As we act, we pray, "O Lord, this seems best; but if it's wrong, forgive me, and by your creative power bring some good out of it."

Trust in the forgiveness and creative possibilities of the Holy Spirit does not reduce our responsibility for careful decision-making, but it does set our choices within the widest perspective of all — the context of the gracious presence of God. Whatever we do, we trust that God is with us, working to bring good out of both our wisdom and our folly.

It may be true, as Paul Sponheim says, that "God can bring more good out of good than he can bring out of evil." But in any case, we have assurance that our worst mistakes do not stop God from loving us nor from opening new possibilities for beginning again. Things may be bad, but "in everything God works for good with those who love him" (Romans 8:28 RSV). When all doors seem closed, his door of grace is still open.

Prayer: O Lord, thank you for loving us through all our blunders. Give us wisdom to choose rightly and lead us beyond our mistakes into new beginnings. In Jesus' name. Amen.

Thought: No mistake takes me beyond new beginnings in God's grace.

Week Thirteen, Day One

1 Corinthians 9:24-27
Hebrews 12:3-13

Stewards Of Self

Jesus took time to be refreshed, and "as good stewards of God's varied grace" (1 Peter 4:10) we are also to care for ourselves. To be sure, we are to neither pamper nor care more for ourselves than others, but we are to keep in shape for God's service.

Such concern is not sinfully selfish. Only as we maintain our spiritual, moral, physical, intellectual, emotional, and social fitness can we be of long-term usefulness to others. We belong not to ourselves but to God and to the "team" of his people sent to work and witness in the world. There is joy in being fit, but that joy is not an end in itself. In athletics the fitness is for victory. In authentic living it is for service that leads to the victory of love over hate, compassion over contempt, life over death. Our fitness is a blessing to others as well as to ourselves.

How much effort should we give to self-improvement? It depends. Students rightly work full-time preparing for a useful vocation, and beyond those years we all need continual self-discipline that fosters growth toward total fitness.

Prayer: O Lord, give us a healthy respect for ourselves and also the wisdom and discipline to keep fit for your service. In Jesus' name. Amen.

Thought: Being good to myself helps me to be better to others.

1 Timothy 4:6-16
1 Thessalonians 5:8-24

Keeping Open To Grace

If life and salvation are all of grace, what is the place of self-discipline in spiritual growth? Our discipline is a response to grace, not a substitute for it. It is giving God and ourselves a chance to function in the harmony for which we are designed.

E. Stanley Jones confessed to being blessed (1) by always having jobs too big for him to do, and (2) by keeping open channels to God's grace. He saw his need and kept open to God's supply.

The chief channels of grace are scripture, sacrament, prayer, fellowship, and service. We read the Bible to receive its gifts. The Good Book is good for us. We wisely ponder at least one passage a day, marking vital insights. Morning and evening prayers of trust, openness, yielding, thanksgiving, and intercession lead to prayerful living throughout the day. Being part of a worshiping, serving community in which word, sacrament, fellowship, and service are shared together, feeds authentic living as food nourishes the body.

Prayer: O Lord, keep us receptive to your grace and give us wisdom to welcome every means by which you seek to bless our lives. In Jesus' name. Amen.

Thought: As I would give strength, I will be open to receive strength.

Week Thirteen, Day Three

Romans 14:1—15:6
1 Corinthians 4:1-5

Never Steal Less Than A Million

"To thine own self be true," said Shakespeare, "and ... thou canst not then be false to any man." Moral fitness involves being true to ourselves and then to others. "Never steal less than a million dollars," said a father to his son; "stealing less is an insult to your character." That advice, when adjusted for inflation, would in practice eliminate most thefts.

"To go against conscience," said Luther, "is neither safe nor right." But unfortunately we can't always let our conscience be our guide. The "weak" conscience may condemn what God blesses (see Romans 14:1—15:6). One "pious" family lived by the rule that "it is all right to smile, but it is a sin to laugh." Others permit laughter but condemn tears. Such is sick religion. On the other extreme, things conscience approves may be "an abomination in the sight of God" (Luke 16:15).

Moral fitness requires guidance beyond the voice of conscience, and we thank God for all that keeps us true to our best selves. Above all, we give thanks for Jesus, who is Lord of conscience, and pray for strength to be Christ-like in act and attitude.

Prayer: O Lord, move us toward moral fitness. Keep our lives in harmony with our humanity and with Christ. In his name. Amen.

Thought: When I am true to Christ, I am most true to myself.

Week Thirteen, Day Four

Romans 7:13-25
1 Corinthians 10:6-13

Willpower?

Paul says, "I can will what is right, but I cannot do it" (Romans 7:18). In one way or another each of us can say, "I do not do the good I want, but the evil I do not want is what I do" (Romans 7:19). Willpower is weak. Our best hope in temptation is to turn to God, who promises to provide "the way of escape" (1 Corinthians 10:13). God-centered trusting, more than self-centered trying, leads to victory.

Yet we are to use all the willpower we have. Paul says, "Shun immorality" (1 Corinthians 6:18); and "aim at righteousness, godliness, faith, love, steadfastness, gentleness" (1 Timothy 6:11).

Satisfaction following a good deed and guilt following a hurtful act reveal that we could have done differently. Limited as it is, our use of willpower in shunning evil and doing good is vital to moral fitness. Yielding to one temptation makes us more vulnerable to the next; choosing the good strengthens us to choose it again. We are not pawns who can say, "The devil made me do it." We are human beings with significant power to will and to act.

Prayer: O Lord, when we are weak, strengthen us. When we are strong, direct us. Enable us to choose the good and do it. In Jesus' name. Amen.

Thought: Yielded to God, my willpower works for good.

Week Thirteen, Day Five

Psalm 103:1-5
1 Thessalonians 5:16-24

Listen To Your Body

Doctors urge us to listen to our bodies. To be sure, our bodies speak with mixed voices. One voice says, "I am hungry; feed me." Another says, "I'm too heavy; stop eating." We wisely heed the voice that speaks for health and, when in doubt, consult a physician.

Proper diet, exercise, rest, and recreation are vital to joyful living. Neglect of health is poor stewardship and hinders our service to others. When willpower fails and eating, drinking, or smoking threatens our health, we surrender our weakness to God's enabling power. If necessary, we yield to a physician's regimen or join a group which supports our own frail resolves.

When weight is a problem, we can become sensuous eaters, savoring every morsel, eating less but enjoying it more. In imagination we see the person we wish to be, and feed on that image rather than on more food. We begin to exercise now as we would after surviving a heart attack. By such discipline we are kind to ourselves so that we can be good to others.

Prayer: O Lord, save us from hurtful habits. Give us wisdom and will to enhance our health. In Jesus' name. Amen.

Thought: When my body speaks for health, I listen and obey.

Week Thirteen, Day Six

Deuteronomy 6:4-10
Philippians 4:8-9

Think About These Things

Our minds, as well as our bodies, need food and exercise. Paul says, "Whatever is true, whatever is honorable, whatever is just, whatever is pure, whatever is lovely, whatever is gracious, if there is any excellence, if there is anything worthy of praise, think about these things" (Philippians 4:8). Such food for thought nourishes a healthy mind. Healthy-mindedness cannot thrive on a diet of trash.

Paul's advice to "think about these things" comes in a context of praise and thanksgiving. When captured by self-pity and bitterness, all we can think about is "poor me" and "terrible you." But as grace begets gratitude, we are enabled to rejoice in all things beautiful.

Jesus states that "you shall love the Lord your God ... with all your mind" (Luke 10:27), and Paul says, "Have this mind among yourselves, which is yours in Christ Jesus" (Philippians 2:5). This is more than healthy-minded religion; it is also healthy-minded humanity. We therefore seek to feed our minds with noble thoughts. We ponder scripture, read the best literature, seek the most inspiring company, and do it all to increase our usefulness as well as our joy. Noble thinking inspires noble living.

Prayer: O Lord, lead us to see all things lovely that abound about us. Fit our minds for greater thoughts. In Jesus' name. Amen.

Thought: No junk for my body; no trash for my mind!

Week Thirteen, Day Seven

Philippians 1:3-11
Romans 12:3-19

With An Open Hand

Stewardship of self includes keeping personal relationships in good repair. Of these relationships one wisely said: "What we need to do, is to hold each other tightly with an open hand."

Love holds tightly — as friends, husbands, wives, children, parents. We hold tightly enough to endure hurt and insult. An unkind word is painful but does not sever the relationship.

But love holds "with an open hand." It does not selfishly coerce or manipulate. Love remembers that "we don't make the beans grow by pulling on them." It gives others freedom to be themselves and to make their own mistakes. Love listens and seeks to understand. It is slow to criticize and explains another's actions in the kindest way.

In parenting and marriage it is difficult to balance holding on and letting go. It helps to remember that this is the way God holds us. He promises never to let us go and yet gives us freedom to act against his will. In such love, we see the pattern for our life together.

Prayer: O Lord, give us love and wisdom to care but not control, to release but not forsake. In Jesus' name. Amen.

Thought: Love holds tightly, but with an open hand.

Week Fourteen, Day One

Isaiah 26:3-4
Philippians 4:4-7

The Gift Of Peace

Few would argue with Norman Cousins that "the most prevalent — and, for all we know, most serious — health problem of our time is stress." To be sure, there never has been an age of tranquility. Jesus said much about triumph over anxiety, and his message has been meaningful for 21 centuries. Yet, we see the effects of stress as never before and do not protest being labeled "the age of anxiety."

We live in stressful situations, but whatever the outer circumstances, our inner response is still crucial. What happens to us is not as important as what happens in us. Pressures are never the whole story; we live in the Divine Presence and are promised "the peace of God, which passes all understanding" (Philippians 4:7). God's gift of serenity can be the prevailing atmosphere of our lives. We are created not for perpetual tension, but for the prevailing calm of the presence of God. In Christ his gift of peace is ours.

Prayer:

Dear Lord and Father of mankind
Forgive our foolish ways ...
Take from our souls the strain and stress,
And let our ordered lives confess
The beauty of thy peace. Amen.

Thought: God's serenity in exchange for my stress? It's a deal!

Week Fourteen, Day Two

Psalm 23:1-6; 46:1-11
Philippians 4:10-13

Born To Trouble

Job's comforters give doubtful counsel, but it is hard to deny that "human beings are born to trouble just as sparks fly upward" (Job 5:7 NRSV) Jesus said the same: "In the world you have tribulation" (John 16:33).

The peace of God is not absence of trouble. Many despised Jesus and desired his death. Paul confessed, "We were so utterly, unbearably crushed that we despaired of life itself" (2 Corinthians 1:8), and later lists many troubles, including imprisonment, beatings, shipwreck, hunger, and thirst (2 Corinthians 11:23-29).

Though the first Christians had much trouble, their lives reflect serenity and joy. What is their secret? Paul answers, "I have learned the secret of facing plenty and hunger, abundance and want. I can do all things in him who strengthens me" (Philippians 4:12-13). Peace came from trust in the power of Christ. Paul lived with the confidence of the Psalmist: "Even though I walk through the valley of the shadow of death, I fear no evil; for thou art with me" (Psalm 23:4). Evil is to be feared, but God is with us and he will bring us through. In his presence is our peace.

Prayer: O Lord, give us ears of faith to hear you say, "Be still, and know that I am God" (Psalm 46:10). In Jesus' name. Amen.

Thought: I may be "born to trouble," but I live to God.

Week Fourteen, Day Three

John 10:22-30
Isaiah 40:10, 11

Being Held

Remember being held in arms of love? This is one picture of God's care for us: "The eternal God is your dwelling place, and underneath are the everlasting arms" (Deuteronomy 33:27). Isaiah says of God, "He will feed his flock like a shepherd, he will gather the lambs in his arms, he will carry them in his bosom" (Isaiah 40:11). Jesus says, "They shall never perish, and no one shall snatch them out of my hand" (John 10:28).

Our peace comes from being held in the arms of God. Storms will surge and fears rise within; yet we are safe in the love of God. He promises to keep and hold us forever.

Being held does not change everything. The world is still the same. But being held changes us. We are different, and the world looks different, too. Now we live with confidence and hope. A mighty peace invades our lives and gives us courage to face troubles we could not face alone. This is, as Paul says, "the peace of God, which passes all understanding" (Philippians 4:7).

Prayer:

O Love that wilt not let me go,
I rest my weary soul in thee;
I give thee back the life I owe,
That in thine ocean depths its flow
May richer, fuller be. Amen.

Thought: My peace is the gift of his presence.

Week Fourteen, Day Four

Acts 26:19-23
Ephesians 4:17-24

Faith Is Not Enough

The peace of God does not automatically cure us of all destructive stress. We may also need to change our way of life. Imagine the stress of being wired to an electric shock device that gives a surprise jolt ten times a day. The real solution to this problem is not just to trust and pray, but to get disconnected from that dreadful machine.

We need more than faith in God. We need to be disconnected from everything that creates hurtful stress. Are we exchanging health for wealth? Is our job destroying our life? Is someone driving us to distraction? Is the chemical balance of our bodies out of order? If so, can something be changed? Can we change our goals or our job? Should we see a counselor or doctor? Begin a diet or start to exercise? Sometimes nothing can be changed. Then we ask strength to endure and to triumph over trouble. But many things can be changed, and we rightly pray for the wisdom and courage to change them.

Prayer: "God, give us grace to accept with serenity the things that cannot be changed, courage to change the things that should be changed, and the wisdom to distinguish the one from the other. Amen."

Thought: Not "grin and bear it" but "grasp and change it" is my motto for today.

Matthew 6:25-34
John 16:32-33

Let God Worry About It

Worrying about everything is a sign of lack of trust in God. We can rightly let God worry. If this seems irresponsible, remember the invitation: "Cast all your anxieties on him, for he cares about you" (1 Peter 5:7).

At wedding rehearsals I suggest that couples let me worry during the wedding. That's my job. In Jesus, God says in effect: "It's my job to be God for you. Don't worry about anything I have promised to provide."

With thankful trust we therefore let God worry about our salvation — he has promised to save us; about our ability to do his will — he assures us of strength enough for that; about what may happen tomorrow — he says, "I will be with you" (Exodus 3:12); about the vital essentials of life — they will be provided even unto resurrection and life eternal.

When Jesus prayed, "Father, into thy hands I commit my spirit!" (Luke 23:46), he not only, as Gerhard Frost says, "taught us everything we need to know about how to die," but also showed us the most essential thing we need to know about how to live.

Prayer: O Lord, keep us mindful of our responsibilities and give us faith to leave the rest to you. In Jesus' name. Amen.

Thought: I will let God be God for me.

Week Fourteen, Day Six — Matthew 10:24-33; 26:36-46

Our Proper Worries

While wishing to escape all hurtful stress, we do not seek to avoid what Rollo May has called "the anxiety of freedom and personal responsibility." With Dr. May we affirm the kind of religious understanding that enhances human "dignity and worth" and "which gives ... a basis for acceptance of normal anxiety."

Healthy dependence on our God brings peace with him and peace within. But it does not free us from the tensions of living and loving in a sinful world. Trust enables life and awakens awareness of responsibility to others. Those who live in the peace of God experience the stress of responsible, authentic humanity in ways unknown to less concerned persons.

Sick dependency abdicates personal freedom and responsibility in exchange for the mistaken belief that God will now decide and do everything for us. God does his work, but he also gives us our work, which neither he nor any other can do for us. The same Jesus who says, "Come to me ... and I will give you rest" (Matthew 11:28), also says, in effect, "Go for me and get to work" (Matthew 28:19). The healthy tension that goes with such responsibility is a sign of life and of love.

Prayer: O Lord, free us from sinful anxiety and give us courage to endure the stress of responsible freedom. In Jesus' name. Amen.

Thought: I depend on God, and God depends on me.

Feed On The Promises

To grow in serenity we feed on the promises of God. At first we rest in silence, doing nothing, but breathing deeply and letting down the weight of our cares upon God as we let down the weight of our bodies upon a chair. Then we turn to promises, like our scriptures for this week, and others such as these: "The Lord is my light and my salvation; whom shall I fear? The Lord is the stronghold of my life; of whom shall I be afraid?" (Psalm 27:1). "Thou dost keep him in perfect peace, whose mind is stayed on thee, because he trusts in thee. Trust in the Lord for ever, for the Lord God is an everlasting rock" (Isaiah 26:3, 4).

The promises sink in, and become part of us. We pray — yielding, trusting, asking only that God's will of love be done in us and through us. His peace begins to prevail. His serenity subdues our stress.

Jesus sought solitude. When crowds pressed upon him, Jesus "withdrew to the wilderness and prayed" (Luke 5:16). If he had time for that, so do we.

Prayer: O Lord, you promise that "in quietness and in trust shall be your strength" (Isaiah 30:15). Give us solitude in which to find such strength. In Jesus' name. Amen.

Thought: Promises provide peace; peace promotes productivity.

Week Fifteen, Day One

Mark 8:34-37
Romans 6:5-14

Abandonment In Action

"Why don't you oil that squeaky fan?" he asked. "I can't; it has sealed bearings," I replied. "Let's look," he said. We looked and, sure enough, there were places to oil. In a few minutes a fan that had been squeaking for weeks was running smoothly.

My failure to do anything about an obvious problem illustrates how we often live with difficulties and never attempt to correct them. There are problems we can't solve, but let's not give up without looking for solutions.

Living by grace relates to every aspect of life. Many perplexing problems can be corrected when we see them in the light of Jesus and learn to live with abandonment. This week we consider six examples of such abandonment in action.

It is naive to suppose that everything from insomnia to sexual dysfunction can be cured by trusting instead of trying, but many troubles either disappear or cease to be problems for us when we cease trying to conquer them on our own. Self-centered attempts to produce spontaneous responses are notoriously counterproductive. When we let go, we not only let God — we also let our minds and bodies function as they were designed to do.

Prayer: O Lord, in every detail of daily living, teach us to live by grace. In Jesus' name. Amen.

Thought: Self-saving stifles; self-losing liberates.

Week Fifteen, Day Two

Exodus 4:10-17
Mark 7:31-37

Speech

In childhood I thought that stuttering was the only problem in the world. Yet I never stuttered when I talked with the dog. Why not? Because the dog did not care. "Stuttering," says Wendell Johnson, "is what a person does to keep from stuttering." It happens when we try too hard to speak fluently and may begin when anxious people call attention to normal repetitions in a child's speech.

The paradoxical cure for stuttering is to quit trying to stop stuttering. This is easier to advocate than to do. It happens only with assurance that we need not speak with perfect fluency and that we will speak better when we quit trying so hard to do so. The specific therapies of speech correction help us to instill this assurance.

Once again, victory comes not through struggle but through surrender — not surrender *to* the problem but surrender *of* the problem. Through abandonment of counterproductive self-saving efforts to speak perfectly, the mental and physical components of speech are freed to function smoothly. Tense and struggling, we stutter all the more. Yielded and relaxed, we speak as freely with people as with the dog.

Prayer: Thank you, Lord, for the gift of speech. Enable us to say all that needs to be said. In Jesus' name. Amen.

Thought: Yielded we are free; struggling we are slaves.

Week Fifteen, Day Three

Psalm 4:1-8; 127:1, 2
Mark 4:26-29, 35-41

Sleep

It's 2 a.m., and we must be up at 6:00. We try to sleep, but the harder we try, the more wakeful we are. Then we give up and reconcile ourselves to being awake all night. Soon we are sound asleep.

Some therapists encourage insomniacs to try to stay awake and may prescribe a notebook to jot down the hours of the night. Other therapists assure people that they need not sleep but can rest as well while awake. In either case, the person is freed from the demand to sleep, and is now open to receive sleep as a gift. In theological terms the shift is from living under the law to living under grace.

Jesus said: "The kingdom of God is as if a man should scatter seed upon the ground, and should sleep and rise night and day, and the seed should sprout and grow, he knows not how. The earth produces of itself, first the blade, then the ear, then the full grain in the ear" (Mark 4:26-28). The wise farmer lets the grain grow of itself. So also, as we live in the grace of God we trust sleep to come of itself without our working at it.

Prayer: "In peace I will both lie down and sleep; for thou alone, O Lord, makest me dwell in safety" (Psalm 4:8). In Jesus' name. Amen.

Thought: Sleep, like salvation, is not my achievement, but God's gift.

Week Fifteen, Day Four

John 5:17; 9:3-4
1 Corinthians 15:8-11

Work

We are created in the image of a working God and through useful work are blessed and give blessing to others. Some fail at work because they do not try hard enough. Others try so hard to do something great, that they fail to even do something small.

A professional man was overwhelmed with the literature in his field. He bought everything, but read little and was plagued by guilt and fear over failure to keep up. Seeing himself under the tyranny of an impossible ideal, he gave up trying to read everything and decided to read only a few books and articles of most importance. Six months later he was amazed to have read more than ever before.

Many urge us to "think big," and it is well to have high aspirations. But it is also important to learn to "think small" — to zero in on one little task and see it through, remembering that as God wills our work, he gives us strength to do it. Then we can say with Paul, "I worked harder than any of them, though it was not I, but the grace of God which is with me" (1 Corinthians 15:10).

Prayer: O Lord, show us a little task for today and give us the initiative and perseverance to do it. In Jesus' name. Amen.

Thought: I work by grace and not by grit, with God and not for glory.

Week Fifteen, Day Five

1 Corinthians 13:1-13
Colossians 3:12-17

Sex

There is a profound connection between grace and sexual fulfillment. Many problems of sexual dysfunction arise not from physical inadequacy but from preoccupation with performance. Sexual ability and satisfaction are not achieved by frantic striving. When preoccupied with performance, our cluttered minds crowd out the stimuli which are creative of fulfillment. When we let go and let ourselves love and be loved, the responses often come of themselves.

That we are saved by grace and not by our own good works applies to sexual fulfillment as well as to salvation. From all that is written about sexual problems, it appears that millions are trying to save themselves sexually by their "good works" and are experiencing great frustration in the process.

Sexually, as every other way, we are created to live by grace. Grace loves without demanding anything. In a gracious sexual relationship there are no demands of one's self or of the other. It is a time for being good to each other, freely giving and receiving tender love and affection. To many who have been fearful and frustrated, the fulfillment enabled by such grace seems a miracle of joy.

Prayer: O Lord, give us love to be gracious in every aspect of our lives together. In Jesus' name. Amen.

Thought: Sex is not a work to perform, but a gift to share.

Week Fifteen, Day Six

Luke 15:11-24
Philippians 1:3-11

In Troubled Relationships

In courtship, marriage, and parenting we may try to coerce a love response from someone for whom we care so much. In crisis situations one person, feeling stifled, may seek freedom to grow. The other, fearful of loss, redoubles efforts to keep and to control. Such efforts, too, are counterproductive. Trying to compel love may destroy it all together.

"I can't live without you" sounds like a tribute of love, but total dependence upon another person is neither healthy nor wise. It is, in fact, a form of idolatry. Only God is worthy of such a place in our lives.

We live best with people we could live without. There are times to say, "I love you so much I will let you go if you don't want to be with me," or "I want you to stay, but I could live without you. The love we have shared will, if necessary, help me go on alone." Such attitudes, which reflect abandonment in action, not only let others be true to themselves but also give them freedom to respond with the authentic love we sometimes too desperately seek. Letting go in love permits, and often helps create, a love response in return.

Prayer: O Lord, thank you for love that gives us freedom. Give us courage to care with liberating love. In Jesus' name. Amen.

Thought: Letting go in love lets others leave, or freely love.

Week Fifteen, Day Seven 1 Corinthians 10:12-13
2 Corinthians 12:1-10

The A. A. Way

The twelve-step program of Alcoholics Anonymous has been adapted for the spouses and the children of alcoholics, for others who are chemically dependent, and also for gamblers, overeaters, the emotionally disturbed, stutterers, parents fearful of harming their children, troubled families, and probably more of which I am not aware. In whatever form, the "A. A. Way" illustrates abandonment in action.

A famous poster pictures a desperate cat clinging by his front paws. The caption reads, "Hang in there, Baby!" Such is not the A. A. Way. Their posters say, "Let Go and Let God."

A. A. works because it is grounded in reality. This way of life confesses our weaknesses and, without being explicitly Christian or even specifically religious about it, affirms the Christian conviction that there is a "Power greater than ourselves" that works to give us life. As God may wish to teach A. A. people more of our theology, he must want to give many of us more of their trust. They know what Paul meant when he said, "When I am weak, then I am strong" (2 Corinthians 12:10).

Prayer: Thank you, Lord, for being the strength of all who trust in you. In Jesus' name. Amen.

Thought: I live not as a clinging cat, but as a trusting child.

Week Sixteen, Day One

Psalm 90:1-12
2 Corinthians 4:7-18

Perpetual Renewal

Whitehead's phrase "perpetual perishing" rings a responsive cord. We see it, feel it, and even sing about it:

Swift to its close ebbs out life's little day;
Earth's joys grow dim, its glories pass away;
Change and decay in all around I see ...

With aging, we lose the vitality of youth and become increasingly conscious of the brevity of life. "Even to live 100 years," said a grieving widower, "is not to live very long."

While realistic about "perpetual perishing," the Bible resounds with hope and joy. "We do not lose heart," says Paul. "Though our outer nature is wasting away, our inner nature is being renewed every day" (2 Corinthians 4:16). In Christ we believe in perpetual renewal. Every morning brings a new day full of the possibilities of the grace of God. We abide in God, and by his power we "look not to the things that are seen but to the things that are unseen; for the things that are seen are transient, but the things that are unseen are eternal" (2 Corinthians 4:18).

Prayer:
Abide with me; fast falls the eventide;
The darkness deepens; Lord with me abide!
When other helpers fail and comforts flee,
Help of the helpless, O abide with me.
Amen.

Thought: My mood springs from the renewing Spirit of Christ.

Week Sixteen, Day Two

Romans 15:1-13
2 Corinthians 1:8-11

Surprises Of The Spirit

"I'd have never believed it," said a widow several months after a tragic loss. "God has given me strength and hope beyond anything I dared to dream. His promise is true: 'As your days, so shall your strength be' " (Deuteronomy 33:25). Millions witness to similar renewal by the Spirit. Life had seemed over. There was nothing to which to look forward but loneliness, grief, pain, and death. But those expectations proved false. The gloom was lifted as if by an unseen mighty hand. There were still people who loved and others who needed loving. There were visits to make, letters to write, prayers to pray, deeds to do; there were even songs to sing and new joys to know.

God doesn't give us a lifetime of strength in a single day. But he does promise: "I will never fail you nor forsake you! Hence we can confidently say, 'The Lord is my helper, I will not be afraid. What can anyone do to me?' " (Hebrews 13:5-6 NRSV). With such expectant confidence we welcome the surprises of the Spirit.

Prayer: Thank you, Lord, for changing our endings into your new beginnings. Bring us daily into new hope and helpfulness. In Jesus' name. Amen.

Thought: My gloom does not cancel the goodness and glory of God.

Ecclesiastes 3:1-15
Jude 24, 25

Making Friends With Time

Some view time as a possession which is being steadily diminished. Every day we are robbed of another 24 hours, and in terms of time are literally becoming poorer by the minute.

But from the perspective of grace, time is not our possession but God's gift. Each moment is an added blessing — a gift from God; who is continually creating more time. Every new minute adds to the treasury of time God gives us to enjoy. With this attitude, we greet the dawn, saying, "This is the day which the Lord has made; let us rejoice and be glad in it" (Psalm 118:24).

Instead of clutching at time to keep it, we open our hands to receive new moments as the gift of God. Letting go of time, we let God give us the time we need. As his gift, time comes to us as a friend rather than fleeing from us as an enemy. And when the gift of time has passed, the gift of eternity in God's greater light and nearer love still stands before us.

Prayer: Thank you, Lord, for the gift of time and the promise of eternity. Give us hope to live with great expectations. In Jesus' name. Amen.

Thought: My time is not running out, but flowing in.

2 Corinthians 5:1-10
Ephesians 3:14-21

We Are Being Prepared

Our "slight momentary affliction," says Paul, "is preparing for us an eternal weight of glory beyond all comparison" (2 Corinthians 4:17).

When such blessing seems beyond belief, Paul reminds us that it is God's doing and that he "is able to do far more abundantly than all that we ask or think" (Ephesians 3:20). What is impossible for us is possible with God.

As the unborn child in the dark silence of the womb is fitted with eyes for light and ears for sound, so we are now endowed with hearts and minds that give "intimations of immortality." We are created for the fullness of life with God. In trust of Christ and "the power of his resurrection" (Philippians 3:10) we live and die, trusting that this world is the womb of life eternal.

Prayer: Eternal Father, give us faith to trust that "neither death, nor life ... nor things present, nor things to come ... nor anything else in all creation, will be able to separate us from the love of God in Christ Jesus our Lord" (Romans 8:38, 39). In his name. Amen.

Thought: Beyond the problems of my present are the possibilities of God's future.

Week Sixteen, Day Five

John 11:21-27
1 Corinthians 15:20-28

The Final Healing

E. Stanley Jones spoke of our resurrection as "the final healing" — of all diseases and deformities that distress and distort our lives, healing from death, healing into the wholeness of greater life in the presence of God.

Sickness and death are neither the intended nor ultimate will of God for us. Only Christ-like, life-giving deeds of love are "acts of God." Why God permits so much that he does not desire is, in part, a tribute to human freedom, and beyond that, a mystery yet to be revealed.

In Christ we trust that God is on the side of life and that he wills us to work with him to eliminate all that is life-degrading and to enhance all that is life-enriching. And then, seeing the resurrection of Christ as a demonstration of God's will and victory over "the last enemy" (1 Corinthians 15:26), we dare believe that our prayers for health and wholeness are not cancelled by death, but will be answered in the healing of resurrection.

Prayer: O Lord, keep us in confidence that our lives are in your hand and that we will be yours forever. In Jesus' name. Amen.

Thought: Even death is not beyond the healing of the Spirit.

Week Sixteen, Day Six

John 14:1-7
1 Peter 1:3-9

A Place For Growing

"We know about as much about heaven as an unhatched chicken knows about a hen house." That is a helpful corrective to arrogant speculation, but it's not quite true. We know Jesus. Jesus' promise to "go and prepare a place" for us evokes our hope: "I will come again and will take you to myself, that where I am you may be also" (John 14:3).

Jesus expands our expectations toward the possibilities of the power of God. As we trust God now for the life we know, we trust him also for life beyond our knowing. "No eye has see, nor ear heard, nor the human heart conceived, what God has prepared for those who love him" (1 Corinthians 2:9 NRSV) In Christ we trust that heaven is prepared for the eternal growth of all God's children.

Having tasted life in grace, we venture on, "looking to Jesus the pioneer and perfecter of our faith" (Hebrews 12:2). In life and in death, we look toward joyful living yet to be.

Prayer: O Lord, bring us and all your children to fullness of life in your presence. Thank you for this great hope. In Jesus' name. Amen.

Thought: "We are God's children now; it does not yet appear what we shall be, but ... we shall be like him, for we shall see him as he is" (1 John 3:2).

Week Sixteen, Day Seven 1 Corinthians 15:51-58
Hebrews 13:20-21

Therefore...!

With eternal hope we rejoice with Paul, saying, "Thanks be to God, who gives us the victory through our Lord Jesus Christ" (1 Corinthians 15:57). But yet there is more! Having proclaimed our resurrection hope, Paul says, "Therefore, my beloved, be steadfast, immovable, always excelling in the work of the Lord, because you know that in the Lord your labor is not in vain" (1 Corinthians 15:58 NRSV).

Paul sees the coming resurrection, far from being an incentive to laziness or disdain of this world, as undergirding the eternal significance of every day and deed. Our lives count; our actions matter even unto eternity. Therefore, his final word is a call not to rest or even to rejoicing, but to get to work. As God never retires, neither should we. Having completed our occupation, we still have our vocation in Christ. He calls us to give ourselves with lifelong abandon to love, pray, work, and witness. In him each day is another step in the adventure of trust and love that is joyful living.

Prayer: O Lord, lead us continually out of ourselves into new ventures of faith, hope, and love. Empower us to be the persons we are born to be and to live the lives we are designed to live. In Jesus' name. Amen.

Thought: I am on the way of grace and, by grace, this is my life forever.

By Grace Through Faith

A Song For Our Venture Of Living

By grace through faith we rest within thy love,
Trust in thy pardon, look to thee above;
Welcomed by thee, we gladly are thine own,
With thankful hearts we bow before thy throne.

By grace through faith we're held in love's embrace,
And in our sin dare gaze upon thy face;
Hold us then, Lord, in arms of mercy strong,
That we with joy may lift to thee our song.

In graceful power, all thine, our strength we find,
For thou in love art mighty, good, and kind;
Enabled thus to give ourselves away,
We yield our all to trust, to serve, obey.

We love because we first are loved by thee,
Now all our thoughts are not of "mine" and "me";
Freed from the bondage of our selfish greed,
We turn to see, to meet some other's need.

By grace through faith we live, and also die,
Raised then by thee to greater life on high;
In that full life beyond the lonely grave,
We once again will praise thy power to save.

This hymn, by the author, may be sung to the tune of "Abide With Me." It is based on "For by grace you have been saved through faith, and this is not your own doing; it is the gift of God — not the result of works, so that no one may boast. For we are what he has made us, created in Christ Jesus for good works, which God prepared beforehand to be our way of life" (Ephesians 2:8-10 NRSV).